# The Joy of Less

Embrace Simplicity for a Happy &
Fulfilled Life

## Dr Bhaskar Bora

**Table of Contents**

- Nurturing relationships without materialism
- Story: The Dalai Lama's teachings on compassion
- Practical tips for building relationships

Chapter 11: Embracing Nature
- The role of nature in a simple life
- Benefits of connecting with nature
- Story: John Muir's love for nature
- Practical tips for embracing nature

Chapter 12: Simple Living in a Modern World
- The balance between modernity and simplicity
- Lessons from Henry David Thoreau's Walden
  Pond experiment
- Adapting simple living principles in the
contemporary era
- Practical tips for modern simple living

Chapter 13: The Power of Gratitude
- Importance of gratitude in simple living
- Practicing gratitude daily
- Story: Oprah Winfrey's gratitude practices
- Practical tips for cultivating gratitude

Chapter 14: Simple Parenting
- Benefits of simple and frugal parenting
- Raising children with values of simplicity
- Story: The parenting approach of the Amish
  community
- Practical tips for simple parenting

Chapter 15: Frugality and Creativity
- How frugality fosters creativity

- Creative solutions for a frugal lifestyle
- Story: J.K. Rowling's journey before fame
- Practical tips for creative frugality

Chapter 16: Simple Work and Productivity
- Benefits of simplicity in work
- Strategies for increasing productivity through simplicity
- Story: Tim Ferriss's approach to work-life balance
- Practical tips for simple productivity

Chapter 17: Travel and Simple Living
- Traveling simply and frugally
- Enjoying travel without extravagance
- Story: Rick Steves' travel philosophy
- Practical tips for simple travel

Chapter 18: Simple and Frugal Hobbies
- Benefits of simple hobbies
- Finding joy in frugal hobbies
- Story: Beatrix Potter's love for nature and art
- Practical tips for simple hobbies

Chapter 19: Community and Simple Living
- Importance of community in a simple life
- Building and participating in a supportive community
- Story: Jane Goodall's community-cantered conservation efforts
- Practical tips for community building

Chapter 20: Embracing Simplicity Like Einstein
- Albert Einstein's simple lifestyle

- His philosophy of simplicity and intellectual focus
- Lessons from Einstein's life
- Practical tips for a focused and simple life

Chapter 21: Leonardo da Vinci: Simplicity and Genius
- Da Vinci's minimalist lifestyle
- His philosophy of intellectual and artistic excellence
- Lessons from Da Vinci's life
- Practical tips for embracing simplicity and creativity

Chapter 22: Living a Life of Compassion Like Mother Teresa
- Mother Teresa's selfless service and modest living
- Her philosophy of compassion and humility
- Lessons from Mother Teresa's life
- Practical tips for a compassionate and humble life

Chapter 23: Sustaining a Simple and Frugal Life
- Maintaining simplicity and frugality long term
- Overcoming challenges and setbacks
- Story: Reflecting on the lives of simple living advocates
- Practical tips for sustaining simplicity and frugality

Conclusion
- Recap of the key messages
- Final thoughts on living a simple and frugal life
- Inspirational closing remarks

Prologue
Epilogue
Acknowledgements
Copyright Information
Legal Disclaimer
References

## Prologue: The Joy of Less

In a world that often equates success with material wealth and the relentless pursuit of more, the concept of living simply and frugally can seem counterintuitive. Yet, there is a growing recognition that true happiness and fulfilment are not found in the accumulation of possessions but in the richness of our experiences, relationships, and inner peace. This book, "The Joy of Less: Embrace Simplicity for a Happy & Fulfilled Life," is an invitation to explore a path less travelled but deeply rewarding.

The journey towards simplicity and frugality is not just about reducing our physical belongings; it's about transforming our mindset and redefining our values. It's about stripping away the unnecessary and focusing on what truly matters, allowing us to live more intentionally and mindfully. By embracing simplicity, we create space for joy, creativity, and connection, fostering a life that is not only more manageable but also more meaningful.

Throughout these pages, you will discover the principles and practices that can help you lead a simple and frugal life. From decluttering your home and managing your finances to cultivating mindfulness and nurturing relationships, this book offers practical advice and inspiration drawn from the lives of notable figures who have exemplified the power of simplicity. The stories of Mahatma

Gandhi, Mother Teresa, Leonardo da Vinci, and many others serve as powerful reminders of the profound impact that a simple and dedicated lifestyle can have.

Living simply does not mean living without; rather, it means living with enough—enough to meet our needs, pursue our passions, and contribute to the well-being of others. It means finding contentment and abundance in the everyday moments and learning to appreciate the beauty of less.

Embarking on this journey, I encourage you to keep an open heart and mind. Embrace the challenges and opportunities that come with simplifying your life and remember that every step you take towards simplicity is a step towards greater clarity, peace, and fulfilment. The path to a simple and frugal life is a personal one, and there is no right or wrong way to proceed. Trust in the process and allow yourself the freedom to explore and grow.

"The Joy of Less: Embrace Simplicity for a Happy & Fulfilled Life" is more than just a guide; it is a celebration of the transformative power of simplicity. May it inspire you to declutter your life, nurture your soul, and find joy in the essence of less.

Welcome to the journey of discovering the joy of less.

In a world where the pace of life is accelerating at an unprecedented rate, where consumerism and materialism dominate our daily existence, it can be challenging to find peace and contentment. The constant bombardment of advertisements, the pressure to keep up with societal expectations, and the endless pursuit of more can leave us feeling overwhelmed and disconnected from what truly matters. This book, "Living a Simple and Frugal Life Happily and Peacefully," aims to offer a sanctuary, a guide to help you navigate towards a life of simplicity, frugality, and profound happiness.

The purpose of this book is to inspire and equip you with the knowledge and tools necessary to embrace simplicity and frugality. It's about learning to live with less, but in doing so, gaining so much more—more time, more peace, more happiness. Simplicity is about stripping away the excess, the unnecessary distractions that clutter our lives, and focusing on what truly brings joy and fulfilment. Frugality, on the other hand, is about making wise and mindful choices with our resources, ensuring that we live within our means and appreciate the value of what we have.

Throughout this book, we will explore various aspects of simple and frugal living. We will delve into the stories of renowned personalities who have championed these principles, learn from their experiences, and draw inspiration from their journeys. From Mahatma Gandhi's minimalist lifestyle to Warren Buffett's prudent financial habits, these stories will serve as beacons of wisdom and motivation. We will also uncover practical tips and strategies that you can implement in your daily life to cultivate simplicity and frugality.

One of the key themes we will explore is the profound impact that simplicity and frugality can have on our overall well-being. By embracing these principles, we can reduce stress, improve our mental and physical health, and create a more balanced and harmonious life. We will examine how decluttering our spaces and minds can lead to greater clarity and focus, how mindful consumption can foster a deeper appreciation for what we have, and how prioritizing meaningful relationships can bring more joy and satisfaction.

The importance of simplicity and frugality cannot be overstated in our modern world. At a time when environmental concerns are escalating, and financial instability is a common worry, these principles offer a sustainable and resilient way of living. Simplicity encourages us to reduce our consumption and waste, making more eco-friendly choices that benefit the planet. Frugality teaches us to be resourceful and intentional with our spending, helping us build financial security and independence.

Consider the benefits of living a simple and frugal life. First and foremost, it allows us to reclaim our time. When we are not consumed by the pursuit of material possessions or overwhelmed by a cluttered environment, we can focus on what truly matters. We can invest our time in activities that bring us joy, nurture our passions, and foster our personal growth. We can also dedicate more time to building and nurturing relationships, creating deeper connections with those we care about.

Financial freedom is another significant benefit of simplicity and frugality. By living within our means and making thoughtful financial choices, we can reduce debt, save for the future, and achieve greater financial stability. This freedom allows us to pursue our goals and dreams without the constant worry of financial strain. It also enables us to be more generous, to give back to our communities and support causes that we believe in.

Moreover, a simple and frugal lifestyle promotes mental and emotional well-being. When we are not constantly chasing after the latest trends or comparing ourselves to others, we can find contentment and satisfaction in our own lives. We can appreciate the small, everyday moments of joy and cultivate a sense of gratitude for what we have. This shift in perspective can lead to greater happiness and a more positive outlook on life.

Living a simple and frugal life also fosters a deeper connection with nature and the environment. By reducing our consumption and making more sustainable choices, we can minimize our ecological footprint and contribute to the health of our planet.

This connection with nature can bring a sense of peace and fulfilment, as we align our lives with the natural rhythms of the world around us.

In this book, we will explore practical ways to simplify and live frugally. Each chapter will provide actionable steps and strategies to help you declutter your life, manage your finances wisely, and cultivate habits that lead to lasting happiness. We will look at how to simplify your home, your schedule, and your mind, how to practice mindful consumption, and how to find joy in the simple pleasures of life.

We will also address common challenges and obstacles that can arise on this journey. Transitioning to a simpler, more frugal lifestyle can be daunting, especially in a society that often equates success with material wealth and abundance. But with patience, perseverance, and a clear sense of purpose, it is entirely possible to embrace these principles and reap their many benefits.

As we embark on this journey together, remember that simplicity and frugality are not about sacrifice or deprivation. They are about making conscious choices that lead to a richer, more meaningful life. They are about finding happiness and peace in the things that truly matter—our relationships, our passions, and our connection to the world around us.

Let this book be your guide, your source of inspiration and practical wisdom. Together, we will explore the art of living simply and frugally and discover the joy and contentment that come from a life well-lived.

## Chapter 1: The Essence of Simplicity

In the hustle and bustle of our modern world, simplicity often feels like an elusive concept, a distant dream overshadowed by the demands of daily life. But what if simplicity could become a tangible reality, a guiding principle that shapes our every decision and action? At its core, simplicity is about stripping away the non-essential to focus on what truly matters. It is a conscious choice to prioritize clarity, intention, and purpose over chaos and clutter.

Simplicity is not about deprivation or self-denial; rather, it is a deliberate practice of making space for what enriches our lives. Imagine a garden, overgrown with weeds and tangled vines. The beauty of the flowers and the fruits is obscured by the invasive plants. By removing the weeds and carefully tending to the garden, we allow the natural beauty to flourish. Similarly, when we simplify our lives, we clear away the distractions and make room for growth, joy, and fulfilment.

Historically, the concept of simplicity has been revered and practised by various cultures and philosophies. The ancient Greeks, for example, valued the idea of "ataraxia," a state of serene calmness achieved by living a simple and balanced life. The Stoics, including notable philosophers like Epictetus and Marcus Aurelius, advocated for simplicity as a path to inner peace and virtue. They believed that true happiness comes from within, not from external possessions or achievements.

In Eastern philosophies, simplicity is also a fundamental principle. Taoism, founded by Laozi, emphasizes living in harmony with the Tao, or the natural way of the universe. This involves embracing simplicity, humility, and contentment. The Japanese concept of "wabi-sabi" celebrates the beauty of imperfection and transience, encouraging a simple and mindful approach to life. These ancient teachings remind us that simplicity is not a modern fad but a timeless wisdom that has guided humanity for centuries.

One of the most profound modern examples of living simply is the life of Mahatma Gandhi. Born into a life of relative privilege, Gandhi chose a path of simplicity and self-discipline that became central to his philosophy and activism. His journey toward simplicity was not an immediate transformation but a gradual process of self-discovery and intentional living.

Gandhi's commitment to simplicity was evident in every aspect of his life. He adopted a minimalist wardrobe, often wearing just a loincloth and shawl, which symbolized his solidarity with the poor and his rejection of material excess. His diet was equally simple, consisting mainly of fruits, vegetables, and grains. Gandhi believed that by simplifying his needs, he could focus more on his spiritual and social responsibilities.

His home, the Sabarmati Ashram, was a model of simplicity. It was a place where people lived in harmony, practising self-sufficiency and engaging in community service. The ashram embodied Gandhi's ideals of simple living and high thinking, fostering an environment where individuals could cultivate inner peace and social responsibility.

Gandhi's simplicity extended beyond his personal life to his public endeavours. His approach to social and political change was rooted in nonviolence and civil disobedience, methods that required immense patience, discipline, and clarity of purpose. By living simply, Gandhi was able to maintain a sharp focus on his mission to achieve independence for India and promote social justice.

Gandhi's life teaches us that simplicity is not just about reducing physical possessions but also about cultivating a clear and purposeful mind. It is about aligning our actions with our values and creating a life that reflects our deepest aspirations. His example inspires us to look beyond the superficial and embrace a more meaningful and intentional way of living.

So, how can we incorporate the essence of simplicity into our own lives? The journey to a simpler life begins with small, intentional steps.

Some practical tips you can use to help you get started:

1. Declutter Your Space: Start with your immediate surroundings. Identify items that no longer serve a purpose or bring you joy and let them go. Create a clean and organized environment that fosters calm and clarity. Remember, a cluttered space often leads to a cluttered mind.

2. Prioritize Your Time: Evaluate how you spend your time each day. Are there activities that drain your energy or add unnecessary stress? Consider simplifying your schedule by focusing on tasks that align with your goals and values. Learn to say no to commitments that do not contribute to your well-being.

3. Mindful Consumption: Before making a purchase, ask yourself if the item is truly necessary. Will it add value to your life, or is it an impulse buy? Embrace the idea of quality over quantity. Invest in fewer, higher-quality items that will last longer and serve you better.

4. Simplify Your Diet: A simple diet can lead to better health and well-being. Focus on whole, unprocessed foods that nourish your body. Plan your meals in advance to avoid the temptation of convenience foods. Remember, simplicity in your diet can lead to greater clarity and energy.

5. Digital Detox: In our technology-driven world, it's easy to become overwhelmed by constant notifications and screen time. Set boundaries for

your digital consumption. Designate specific times for checking emails and social media and unplug during meals or before bedtime. A digital detox can help you reconnect with the present moment and reduce stress.

6. Cultivate Gratitude: Practice gratitude by acknowledging the simple blessings in your life. Each day, take a moment to reflect on what you are thankful for. This practice can shift your focus from what you lack to what you have, fostering a sense of contentment and joy.

7. Nurture Relationships: Simplify your social life by focusing on meaningful connections. Invest time in relationships that uplift and inspire you. Let go of toxic or draining relationships that do not contribute to your happiness. Quality relationships can bring immense joy and support.

8. Slow Down: Embrace the art of slow living. Take time to savour your meals, enjoy a leisurely walk, or engage in a hobby that brings you joy. By slowing down, you can appreciate the beauty of the present moment and reduce the stress of constant hurry.

9. Practice Mindfulness: Incorporate mindfulness into your daily routine. Whether it's through meditation, deep breathing, or simply being present in your activities, mindfulness can help you stay grounded and focused. It encourages a deeper connection with yourself and the world around you.

10. Set Clear Goals: Define what simplicity means to you and set clear, achievable goals. Whether it's reducing your possessions, simplifying your schedule, or improving your financial habits, having a clear vision can guide your actions and keep you motivated.

11. Embrace Imperfection: Understand that simplicity is not about achieving perfection. It's about making progress and finding balance. Be gentle with yourself and celebrate small victories along the way. Embrace the journey and learn from each step.

By integrating these practices into your life, you can begin to experience the profound benefits of simplicity. Remember, the journey to a simpler life is unique to each individual. There is no one-size-fits-all approach. What matters is finding what works for you and aligning your actions with your values and aspirations.

The rewards of living simply are manifold. Not only can it lead to greater peace and contentment, but it can also foster a deeper sense of purpose and fulfilment. By choosing simplicity, you are choosing to focus on what truly matters, to live with intention and clarity, and to create a life that reflects your deepest values.

As you embark on this journey of simplicity, let the words of Leonardo da Vinci guide you: "Simplicity is the ultimate sophistication." In a world that often glorifies complexity and excess, simplicity stands as a testament to elegance and wisdom. It is a path that leads to a more meaningful, joyful, and fulfilling life.

Throughout the chapters that follow, we will delve deeper into various aspects of simple and frugal living. We will explore the stories of individuals who have embraced these principles and draw inspiration from their experiences. We will uncover practical tips and strategies that you can apply to your own life, helping you navigate the challenges and reap the benefits of simplicity.

Living simply is not about making drastic changes overnight. It is a gradual process of self-discovery and intentional living. It requires patience, persistence, and a willingness to let go of what no longer serves you. But with each step you take, you will find yourself closer to a life of peace, happiness, and fulfilment.

As you read this book, I encourage you to reflect on your own life and identify areas where you can simplify. Start small, celebrate your progress, and remain open to new possibilities. Remember, the journey to simplicity is a personal one, and there is no right or wrong way to approach it.

May this book be your guide and companion on this journey. May it inspire you to embrace the beauty of simplicity and discover the joy that comes from living a life aligned with your deepest values. May you find peace, happiness, and fulfilment in the simple, everyday moments that make life truly meaningful.

## Chapter 2: Understanding Frugality

Frugality, like simplicity, is often misunderstood. It conjures images of penny-pinching and deprivation, of living a life stripped of joy and indulgence. However, true frugality is not about being miserly or stingy; it is about making wise and intentional choices with our resources. Frugality is the art of living well within our means, prioritizing value over cost, and finding joy in the abundance of what we already have.

At its core, frugality is about resourcefulness and mindfulness. It involves understanding the difference between needs and wants, making thoughtful spending decisions, and appreciating the value of each dollar. Frugality is a path to financial independence and security, allowing us to save for the future, reduce debt, and achieve our financial goals. It is about making the most of what we have, rather than constantly striving for more.

The distinction between frugality and stinginess is crucial. While stinginess is characterized by an unwillingness to spend even when necessary, frugality is about spending wisely. A frugal person may invest in high-quality items that last longer, rather than opting for the cheapest option available. They understand that true value is not always reflected in the price tag. Frugality is about balance, about making choices that reflect our values and goals, rather than mindlessly cutting costs at every turn.

Frugality is also deeply connected to the concept of sustainability. By consuming less and making thoughtful choices, we reduce our impact on the environment. We learn to appreciate the resources we have and find creative ways to use them more efficiently. This approach not only benefits our personal finances but also contributes to a more sustainable and equitable world.

One of the most well-known examples of frugality in the modern world is Warren Buffett, one of the richest men on the planet. Despite his immense wealth, Buffett is known for his modest lifestyle and frugal habits. His story serves as a powerful testament to the value of living simply and wisely, regardless of one's financial status.

Warren Buffett still lives in the house he bought in Omaha, Nebraska, in 1958 for $31,500. This unpretentious, five-bedroom home is a stark contrast to the lavish mansions typically associated with billionaires. Buffett has often stated that he has everything he needs in this house, demonstrating that happiness and comfort do not necessarily come from extravagant living.

Buffett's frugality extends beyond his home to his daily habits. He famously starts his day with a simple breakfast from McDonald's, spending no more than $3.17. He prefers to drive himself around in a modest car and eschews luxury items and lavish vacations. His frugal lifestyle allows him to focus on what he values most: his work, his family, and his philanthropy.

Buffett's approach to investing also reflects his frugal mindset. He is known for his value investing strategy, seeking out companies that are undervalued by the market but have strong fundamentals. This long-term, disciplined approach has allowed him to amass significant wealth while minimizing risk. Buffett's philosophy of "buying quality at a reasonable price" applies not just to his investments but to his entire way of life.

The lessons from Warren Buffett's frugality are clear: living modestly and making wise financial decisions can lead to both personal satisfaction and financial success. His example challenges the notion that wealth must be flaunted, and that happiness comes from constant consumption.

Adopting a frugal lifestyle can be a transformative experience. It begins with a shift in mindset, recognizing that true wealth is not measured by material possessions but by financial security, personal freedom, and a sense of contentment. Here are some practical tips to help you embrace frugality:

1. Track Your Spending: The first step to adopting frugality is understanding where your money goes. Keep a detailed record of your expenses for a

month. This exercise can be eye-opening, revealing areas where you might be overspending or wasting money. Once you have a clear picture of your spending habits, you can identify opportunities to cut back.

2. Create a Budget: A budget is a powerful tool for managing your finances. Start by listing your monthly income and fixed expenses, such as rent, utilities, and insurance. Then allocate funds for variable expenses, like groceries, transportation, and entertainment. Make sure to include a category for savings. A well-planned budget helps you stay on track and ensures that your spending aligns with your financial goals.

3. Distinguish Between Needs and Wants: Before making a purchase, ask yourself if it is a need or a want. Needs are essential for your well-being and daily functioning, while wants are things that would be nice to have but are not necessary. Prioritizing needs over wants can help you make more mindful spending decisions.

4. Embrace DIY: Doing things yourself can save a significant amount of money. Whether it's cooking meals at home, performing basic home repairs, or creating homemade gifts, DIY projects can be both frugal and fulfilling. They also provide an opportunity to learn new skills and enjoy a sense of accomplishment.

5. Seek Out Deals and Discounts: Being frugal doesn't mean never spending money; it means spending wisely. Look for sales, use coupons, and take advantage of discounts whenever possible. However, be mindful of falling into the trap of buying things just because they are on sale. Ensure that your purchases are intentional and necessary.

6. Reduce, Reuse, Recycle: This mantra of sustainability is also a cornerstone of frugality. Reduce your consumption by buying only what you need. Reuse items whenever possible, whether it's repurposing old furniture or using reusable shopping bags. Recycle to minimize waste and make the most of the resources you have.

7. Invest in Quality: While it might seem counterintuitive, spending a bit more upfront for high-quality items can save you money in the long run. Quality products tend to last longer and perform better, reducing the need for frequent replacements. This principle applies to clothing, appliances, furniture, and even food.

8. Limit Impulse Purchases: Impulse buying is a major obstacle to frugality. To curb this habit, implement a waiting period for non-essential purchases. If you see something you want, wait 24 hours before buying it. This pause gives you time to consider whether the item is truly necessary and aligns with your financial goals.

9. Cook at Home: Eating out frequently can quickly drain your budget. Cooking at home is not only more economical but also healthier. Plan your meals, make a shopping list, and prepare food in batches to save time and money. Home-cooked meals can be just as delicious and satisfying as restaurant fare.

10. Find Free or Low-Cost Entertainment: Enjoying life doesn't have to be expensive. Look for free or low-cost activities, such as hiking, visiting local parks, attending community events, or enjoying a good book from the library. Engaging in hobbies and activities that don't cost much can be incredibly fulfilling.

11. Plan for the Future: Frugality is about making wise financial decisions today to secure a better tomorrow. Make saving a priority, even if it's just a small amount each month. Build an emergency fund to cover unexpected expenses and consider investing in your future through retirement accounts or other long-term savings plans.

12. Practice Gratitude: Cultivating a sense of gratitude can shift your focus from what you lack to what you have. Regularly take time to reflect on the blessings in your life, both big and small. This practice can help you find contentment with what you have and reduce the desire for unnecessary purchases.

Adopting frugality is not about living a life of austerity but about making intentional choices that lead to greater financial security and personal fulfilment. It's about finding joy in the simple things and appreciating the value of what you have. By embracing frugality, you can reduce financial stress, achieve your goals, and create a life that reflects your values.

As we continue our exploration of frugality, remember that it is a personal journey. What works for one person may not work for another. The key is to find a balance that aligns with your lifestyle and financial goals. By making small, consistent changes, you can gradually transform your relationship with money and create a more abundant and fulfilling life.

We will delve deeper into specific aspects of frugal living. We will explore how to manage your finances effectively, simplify your diet, find joy in minimalism, and much more. Each chapter will provide practical tips and insights to help you on your journey.

Embrace the essence of frugality with an open heart and mind. Let it guide you towards a life of greater peace, happiness, and financial freedom.
Remember, frugality is not about what you give up; it's about what you gain—security, independence, and the joy of living a life true to your values.

## Chapter 3: Decluttering Your Life

The clutter in our lives often extends beyond the physical, infiltrating our minds and emotions. In a world brimming with distractions, decluttering becomes not just a necessity but a pathway to a clearer, more focused, and more fulfilling life. Decluttering is the process of removing unnecessary items from our surroundings and making space for what truly matters. It is about simplifying our environments to enhance our well-being and productivity.

The importance of decluttering cannot be overstated. A cluttered space can lead to a cluttered mind. Physical clutter creates visual chaos, which can cause stress and anxiety. It can make it difficult to find what we need, leading to frustration and wasted time. Moreover, clutter can impact our mental and emotional health, making it harder to relax and focus.

Decluttering is more than just tidying up; it is about creating an environment that supports our goals and well-being. It allows us to let go of the past and make room for new experiences. By decluttering, we can reduce stress, increase productivity, and create a sense of calm and order in our lives.

Marie Kondo, a Japanese organizing consultant, has become synonymous with the art of decluttering.

Her journey and philosophy have inspired millions around the world to embrace a simpler, more organized life. Kondo's method, known as the KonMari Method, focuses on keeping only those items that "spark joy." This approach encourages individuals to mindfully evaluate their belongings and let go of anything that no longer serves a purpose or brings happiness.

Marie Kondo's journey began at a young age when she discovered her passion for organizing. She spent years studying various organizing techniques and eventually developed her unique approach. Kondo's philosophy is rooted in the belief that a tidy space leads to a tidy mind. By surrounding ourselves with items that spark joy, we can create a home that reflects our true selves and supports our happiness.

The KonMari Method involves a systematic approach to decluttering. Rather than organizing room by room, Kondo recommends decluttering by category. The categories are typically tackled in the following order: clothes, books, papers, miscellaneous items, and sentimental items. This method allows individuals to focus on one type of item at a time, making the process more manageable and effective.

The first step in the KonMari Method is to gather all items in a category in one place. For example, when decluttering clothes, gather all clothing items from every room and closet. This helps you see the sheer volume of items you own and makes it easier to evaluate each one. Hold each item in your hands and ask yourself if it sparks joy. If it does, keep it. If it doesn't, thank the item for its service and let it go. This mindful approach helps create a deeper connection with your belongings and encourages gratitude.

Marie Kondo's philosophy extends beyond physical items to encompass all aspects of life. She believes that by decluttering our homes, we can declutter our minds and hearts, leading to greater clarity and happiness. Her method has transformed countless lives, helping people let go of the unnecessary and embrace what truly matters.

While the KonMari Method is highly effective, there are various other strategies and methods for decluttering. The key is to find an approach that resonates with you and your lifestyle. Here are some additional methods and strategies for decluttering:

1. The Minimalist Game: This method involves getting rid of one item on the first day, two items on the second day, three items on the third day, and so on, for an entire month. By the end of the month, you will have decluttered hundreds of items. This gradual approach makes the process more manageable and can be a fun challenge.

2. Four-Box Method: When decluttering a space, use four boxes labelled: Keep, Donate, Sell, and Trash. As you go through your belongings, place

each item in one of the boxes. This method helps you make clear decisions about each item and provides a plan for what to do with them.

3. One-In, One-Out Rule: To maintain a clutter-free space, adopt the one-in, one-out rule. For every new item you bring into your home, let go of an existing item. This rule helps prevent new clutter from accumulating and encourages mindful consumption.

4. Daily Decluttering Habit: Incorporate a daily decluttering habit into your routine. Spend just 10-15 minutes each day tidying up a specific area or category. Consistent, small efforts can lead to significant results over time.

5. The 90/90 Rule: When evaluating items, ask yourself if you have used the item in the past 90 days and if you plan to use it in the next 90 days. If the answer is no to both questions, it might be time to let go of the item. This rule helps you keep only what is truly useful.

6. Digital Declutter: Clutter is not limited to physical items. Digital clutter, such as unnecessary emails, files, and apps, can also impact your mental space. Regularly clean out your digital devices and organize your files to create a more efficient and focused digital environment.

Decluttering is a personal journey, and there is no one-size-fits-all approach. The key is to start small, be consistent, and stay mindful of your goals. As you declutter, you may find that the process itself brings a sense of relief and accomplishment. Letting go of physical clutter can lead to a greater sense of freedom and clarity, allowing you to focus on what truly matters.

Marie Kondo's story and philosophy have resonated with so many because they tap into a universal desire for order and tranquillity. Her approach is not just about tidying up; it's about creating a home that nurtures your soul and supports your aspirations. By focusing on what sparks joy, we can transform our living spaces into sanctuaries of peace and inspiration.

Beyond the physical benefits, decluttering can have profound psychological and emotional impacts. A decluttered space can lead to reduced stress and anxiety, improved focus and productivity, and a greater sense of control over your environment. When our surroundings are orderly, we can think more clearly and feel more at ease.

Practical decluttering tips are essential to maintaining a clutter-free life. Here are some actionable steps to help you on your decluttering journey:

1. Set Clear Goals: Before you begin decluttering, define your goals. What do you hope to achieve? Whether it's creating a more organized home, reducing stress, or making room for new

experiences, having clear goals will guide your efforts and keep you motivated.

2. Start Small: Decluttering can be overwhelming if you try to tackle everything at once. Start with a small area, such as a drawer or a shelf, and gradually work your way through larger spaces. Celebrate your progress along the way to stay motivated.

3. Create a System: Develop a system that works for you. This might involve setting aside specific times for decluttering, using storage solutions to organize items, or implementing a routine for maintaining a clutter-free space. A consistent system can make the process more manageable.

4. Involve Your Family: If you live with others, involve them in the decluttering process. Encourage each family member to take responsibility for their own spaces and belongings. Working together can make the process more efficient and enjoyable.

5. Let Go of Guilt: It's common to hold onto items out of guilt or obligation, especially if they were gifts or inherited. Remember that your home should reflect your needs and values. If an item no longer serves a purpose or brings joy, it's okay to let it go.

6. Donate and Recycle: Consider donating items that are in good condition to charities or recycling those that can be repurposed. This not only helps others but also aligns with sustainable practices.

Knowing that your items can benefit someone else can make it easier to part with them.

7. Be Mindful of Future Purchases: To prevent future clutter, be mindful of what you bring into your home. Before making a purchase, consider its necessity and how it fits into your life. Embrace quality over quantity and choose items that truly add value.

8. Celebrate Your Progress: Decluttering is an ongoing process, and it's important to acknowledge your achievements along the way. Celebrate your progress, no matter how small, and enjoy the benefits of a more organized and peaceful space.

Decluttering your life is a powerful step towards simplicity and happiness. It allows you to create an environment that supports your well-being and reflects your true self. By letting go of the unnecessary, you can make room for what truly matters and find joy in the simplicity of a clutter-free life.

Decluttering is just one aspect of living a simple and frugal life. Each step you take towards simplicity brings you closer to a life of greater peace, happiness, and fulfilment. Embrace the process, stay mindful of your goals, and enjoy the freedom that comes from a decluttered and intentional life.

## Chapter 4: Financial Wisdom for Simple Living

Financial wisdom is a cornerstone of simple living. By mastering the basics of personal finance, we can achieve a level of security and freedom that allows us to focus on what truly matters. Financial wisdom is not about accumulating wealth for its own sake but about making informed decisions that lead to stability, independence, and peace of mind. It empowers us to live within our means, prepare for the future, and make meaningful choices that align with our values.

The first step towards financial wisdom is understanding the basics of personal finance. This includes knowing how to manage your income, expenses, savings, and investments. At its core, personal finance is about balancing your income with your expenses and ensuring that you are saving for both short-term needs and long-term goals. It involves creating a budget, tracking your spending, and making informed decisions about how to use your money.

Budgeting is a fundamental tool in personal finance. A budget is a plan that outlines your income and expenses over a specific period, usually a month. It helps you ensure that your spending aligns with your financial goals and prevents you from living beyond your means. To create a budget, start by listing all sources of income, such as your salary, side jobs, or investments. Next, list all your expenses, including fixed costs like rent or mortgage, utilities, and insurance, as well as variable costs like groceries, entertainment, and transportation.

Once you have a clear picture of your income and expenses, you can identify areas where you can cut back or save. The goal is to ensure that your expenses do not exceed your income and that you are setting aside money for savings and investments. A well-planned budget can help you reduce debt, save for the future, and achieve your financial goals.

Saving strategies are another crucial aspect of financial wisdom. Saving is the process of setting aside money for future needs or emergencies. It provides a financial cushion that can help you navigate unexpected expenses or opportunities. There are several effective saving strategies you can adopt:

1. Pay Yourself First: This strategy involves setting aside a portion of your income for savings before you pay any other bills. By prioritizing savings, you ensure that you are consistently building your financial security.

2. Automate Savings: Set up automatic transfers from your checking account to your savings

account. This ensures that you save regularly without having to think about it.

3. Create an Emergency Fund: Aim to save at least three to six months' worth of living expenses in an easily accessible account. This fund can help you cover unexpected costs, such as medical bills or car repairs, without going into debt.

4. Save Windfalls: Whenever you receive unexpected money, such as a tax refund, bonus, or gift, consider saving a significant portion of it. This can give your savings a substantial boost.

5. Cut Unnecessary Expenses: Review your budget to identify and eliminate unnecessary expenses. Redirect the money you save towards your savings goals.

One of the most influential figures in the realm of personal finance is Dave Ramsey. Known for his straightforward and practical advice, Ramsey has helped millions of people take control of their finances through his books, radio shows, and financial education programs. His approach to financial wisdom is rooted in common sense and discipline, focusing on getting out of debt, building an emergency fund, and investing for the future.

Dave Ramsey's financial wisdom is encapsulated in his "Seven Baby Steps," a series of progressive steps designed to help individuals achieve financial peace:

1. Baby Step 1: Save $1,000 for a Starter Emergency Fund. This initial fund is a safety net for small emergencies that might otherwise derail your financial progress.

2. Baby Step 2: Pay Off All Debt (Except the House) Using the Debt Snowball. Ramsey advocates for listing all debts from smallest to largest, paying off the smallest first while making minimum payments on the rest. Once a debt is paid off, roll its payment into the next smallest debt. This method builds momentum and motivation as you see your debts disappear one by one.

3. Baby Step 3: Save 3-6 Months of Expenses in a Fully Funded Emergency Fund. This larger fund provides a more substantial buffer against major financial disruptions, such as job loss or significant medical expenses.

4. Baby Step 4: Invest 15% of Your Household Income in Retirement. Ramsey emphasizes the importance of long-term financial security through retirement savings. Contribute to retirement accounts like 401(k)s and IRAs to ensure a comfortable future.

5. Baby Step 5: Save for Your Children's College Fund. If you have children, start saving for their education to minimize the need for student loans and provide them with a debt-free start to their adult lives.

6. Baby Step 6: Pay Off Your Home Early. Once you have addressed other financial priorities, focus on paying off your mortgage to achieve complete financial freedom.

7. Baby Step 7: Build Wealth and Give. With no debts and substantial savings, you can focus on building wealth through investments and enjoy the freedom to be generous with your resources.

Dave Ramsey's approach is powerful because it breaks down the complex task of managing personal finances into manageable, actionable steps. By following these steps, individuals can gain control over their money, reduce financial stress, and build a secure future.

In addition to these steps, Ramsey emphasizes the importance of living on a budget, avoiding debt, and practising contentment. He often reminds his followers that financial success is not about how much you earn but how wisely you manage what you have. His philosophy encourages people to live below their means, avoid lifestyle inflation, and make intentional financial choices that reflect their values.

To adopt financial wisdom in your own life, consider the following practical tips:

1. Create and Stick to a Budget: A budget is your financial roadmap. Review it regularly and adjust it as needed to stay on track with your goals.

2. Avoid Debt: Debt can be a significant obstacle to financial freedom. Avoid taking on new debt and work diligently to pay off existing debts. Use cash or debit cards instead of credit cards to control your spending.

3. Build an Emergency Fund: Having a financial cushion can prevent small emergencies from turning into financial crises. Aim to save at least three to six months of living expenses.

4. Invest Wisely: Start investing as early as possible to take advantage of compound interest. Focus on long-term investments, such as retirement accounts, and diversify your portfolio to reduce risk.

5. Live Below Your Means: Resist the temptation to keep up with others or live beyond your income. Focus on your own financial goals and make choices that support them.

6. Seek Financial Education: Continuously educate yourself about personal finance. Read books, listen to podcasts, and follow financial experts to stay informed and inspired.

7. Plan for Major Expenses: Anticipate and save for significant expenses, such as home repairs,

vacations, or medical costs. Planning ahead can prevent these expenses from derailing your budget.

8. Practice Contentment: Learn to appreciate what you have and avoid comparing yourself to others. Contentment can lead to better financial decisions and greater overall happiness.

9. Give Generously: Financial wisdom includes generosity. Giving to others, whether through charity, supporting loved ones, or contributing to your community, can bring joy and fulfilment.

10. Review and Adjust Your Goals: Regularly review your financial goals and progress. Adjust your plans as needed to stay aligned with your changing circumstances and priorities.

Adopting these practices can help you achieve financial stability and peace of mind. Remember that financial wisdom is a journey, not a destination. It requires ongoing effort, discipline, and a willingness to learn and adapt.

While continuing to explore the principles of simple and frugal living, it's pertinent to remember that financial wisdom is a key component. By managing your finances wisely, you can create a life of greater freedom, security, and happiness. Financial wisdom allows you to focus on what truly matters, freeing you from the stress and constraints of financial insecurity.

Let's delve deeper into more aspects of simple living, from minimalism to sustainable living, and discover how these principles can further enhance your life. By integrating financial wisdom with other elements of simplicity, you can create a holistic approach to living well and finding joy in everyday moments.

Financial wisdom is not just about managing money; it is about making intentional choices that align with your values and goals. It is about creating a life of security and freedom, where you can focus on what truly matters. Whether you are just starting your financial journey or looking to refine your approach, the principles of budgeting, saving, and wise investing can guide you towards a more fulfilling and prosperous life.

Remember the words of Dave Ramsey: "You must gain control over your money, or the lack of it will forever control you." By taking charge of your finances, you can pave the way for a life of greater peace and happiness. Embrace the journey with patience and perseverance and celebrate each step forward as a victory.

As you apply these principles, you will find that financial wisdom enhances every aspect of your life. It empowers you to live with purpose, make meaningful choices, and enjoy the freedom that comes from financial security. Let this chapter be a starting point for your journey towards a simpler, more financially sound life.

Continue to explore the chapters ahead, where we will delve further into the various facets of simple living. Each chapter offers insights and practical tips to help you simplify your life, reduce stress, and find joy in the everyday. Together, we will discover the beauty and fulfilment that come from living simply and wisely.

## Chapter 5: The Joy of Minimalism

In a world overflowing with material possessions and constant distractions, minimalism offers a refreshing alternative. Minimalism is more than just a design aesthetic or a trend; it is a lifestyle that emphasizes the importance of living with less to create more space for what truly matters. By embracing minimalism, we can strip away the excess and focus on the essentials, leading to a life filled with purpose, clarity, and joy.

Understanding minimalism begins with recognizing that it is not about deprivation or austerity. Instead, minimalism is about making intentional choices to reduce the clutter—both physical and mental—that can weigh us down. It is about curating our lives to include only those things that bring us joy and serve a meaningful purpose. Minimalism challenges the pervasive notion that more is always better and encourages us to find contentment with less.

The benefits of minimalistic living are manifold. Firstly, minimalism can lead to greater financial freedom. By reducing our consumption and focusing on what we truly need, we can save money and avoid the cycle of debt and overconsumption. This financial stability allows us to invest in experiences and opportunities that enrich our lives, rather than accumulating material possessions that provide only temporary satisfaction.

Secondly, minimalism promotes mental and emotional well-being. A cluttered environment can lead to a cluttered mind, contributing to stress and anxiety. By simplifying our surroundings, we create a calm and organized space that fosters clarity and peace. Minimalism also encourages mindfulness, as we become more intentional about our choices and actions.

Minimalism also enhances our relationships. When we prioritize experiences and connections over material goods, we create more meaningful interactions with those around us. By spending less time managing and maintaining possessions, we can dedicate more time to nurturing our relationships and building deeper connections.

One of the most compelling stories of minimalism comes from Joshua Fields Millburn and Ryan Nicodemus, known as The Minimalists. Their journey towards minimalism began in 2009 when both were experiencing the trappings of the American Dream—high-paying jobs, luxury cars, and all the material possessions one could desire. Despite their outward success, they found themselves unfulfilled and unhappy.

Millburn and Nicodemus decided to make a radical change. They began by decluttering their homes, getting rid of items that no longer added value to their lives. This process led to a profound transformation, not just in their physical spaces but in their overall well-being. They discovered that by letting go of excess possessions, they could focus on what truly mattered—health, relationships, personal growth, and contribution to others.

Their story resonated with many, leading them to share their experiences through their website, books, and a popular documentary titled "Minimalism: A Documentary About the Important Things." The Minimalists have inspired millions to embrace a simpler, more intentional way of living. Their philosophy is encapsulated in their motto: "Love people, use things. The opposite never works."

Millburn and Nicodemus emphasize that minimalism is not a one-size-fits-all solution. It is a personal journey that looks different for everyone. The key is to identify what is most important to you and to remove anything that distracts from those priorities. This approach allows for greater focus, satisfaction, and a deeper sense of purpose.

For those interested in adopting minimalism, practical tips can be invaluable. Here are some strategies to help you begin your minimalist journey:

1. Start with a Clear Vision: Before you begin decluttering, take some time to define your vision for a minimalist life. What do you hope to achieve? What areas of your life do you want to simplify?

Having a clear vision will guide your efforts and keep you motivated.

2. Declutter Ruthlessly: Go through your belongings and ask yourself if each item serves a purpose or brings you joy. Be honest with yourself and let go of anything that no longer adds value. Remember, the goal is to create a space that supports your well-being and goals.

3. Adopt the "One-In, One-Out" Rule: To maintain a clutter-free environment, practice the "one-in, one-out" rule. For every new item you bring into your home, let go of an existing item. This helps prevent new clutter from accumulating and encourages mindful consumption.

4. Simplify Your Wardrobe: A minimalist wardrobe can save you time, money, and stress. Focus on versatile, high-quality pieces that you love and wear regularly. Consider creating a capsule wardrobe—a small collection of essential items that can be mixed and matched.

5. Limit Digital Clutter: Minimalism isn't just about physical possessions. Digital clutter, such as unnecessary emails, apps, and files, can also overwhelm you. Regularly clean out your digital devices and organize your files to create a more efficient and focused digital space.

6. Be Mindful of Purchases: Before making a purchase, ask yourself if the item is truly necessary

and if it aligns with your minimalist goals. Avoid impulse buys and prioritize quality over quantity. By being mindful of your purchases, you can reduce waste and save money.

7. Focus on Experiences Over Things: Minimalism encourages us to value experiences and relationships over material possessions. Spend your time and money on activities that bring you joy and create lasting memories, such as travel, hobbies, and spending time with loved ones.

8. Practice Gratitude: Cultivating gratitude can help you appreciate what you have and reduce the desire for more. Regularly take time to reflect on the positive aspects of your life and express gratitude for the people and experiences that bring you joy.

9. Create a Daily Routine: Establishing a simple and consistent daily routine can help you stay organized and focused. Prioritize your most important tasks and set aside time for self-care and relaxation. A well-structured routine can reduce stress and increase productivity.

10. Let Go of Perfection: Minimalism is not about achieving a perfect, pristine space. It's about creating a life that is meaningful and fulfilling. Embrace the imperfections and focus on progress, not perfection. Allow yourself the flexibility to adjust and adapt your minimalist practices as needed.

Adopting minimalism is a personal journey that requires patience and perseverance. It involves letting go of old habits and embracing new ways of thinking. As you begin to simplify your life, you may find that the process itself brings a sense of relief and liberation. By removing the excess, you create space for clarity, creativity, and joy.

Minimalism aligns with sustainable living too. By consuming less and making mindful choices, we reduce our impact on the environment. Minimalism encourages us to be more resourceful and intentional, promoting a lifestyle that is both fulfilling and eco-friendly.

The joy of minimalism lies in its ability to transform our lives. It allows us to break free from the constant pursuit of more and find contentment with what we have. By focusing on what truly matters, we can create a life that is rich in purpose and meaning.

Forging ahead in our journey through this book, we should remember that minimalism is not about deprivation but about liberation. It is about creating a life that reflects your values and brings you joy. Embrace the process with an open heart and mind and allow yourself to experience the profound benefits of living with less.

In the following chapters, we will explore more aspects of simple living, from sustainable practices to mindful consumption. Each chapter will provide practical tips and insights to help you simplify your life and find happiness in the everyday moments. Together, we will discover the beauty and fulfilment that come from living simply and intentionally.

Minimalism is a powerful tool for creating a more intentional and fulfilling life. By understanding its principles and embracing its practices, you can transform your environment, your mindset, and your overall well-being. The journey to minimalism is unique for each individual, and it begins with a single step—choosing to live with less so that you can focus on more.

As you apply the strategies and tips outlined in this chapter, note that minimalism is not a destination but an ongoing process. It requires continuous reflection and adjustment, as you discover what works best for you and your lifestyle. Celebrate your progress, no matter how small, and remain committed to your vision of a simpler, more meaningful life.

The story of The Minimalists, Joshua Fields Millburn and Ryan Nicodemus, is a powerful reminder that minimalism is not about what you own but what you value. Their journey from corporate success to a minimalist lifestyle highlights the profound impact that simplicity can have on our happiness and well-being.

As you continue exploring simple living principles in this book, remember that minimalism is just one aspect of a larger philosophy. It complements practices such as frugality, mindfulness, and sustainable living, creating a holistic approach to a more intentional and joyful life.

Let this chapter be a guide and inspiration for your minimalist journey. Embrace the joy of living with less and discover the freedom and fulfilment that come from focusing on what truly matters. Together, we will explore the many facets of simple living, uncovering the beauty and happiness that lie within a life of intentional simplicity.

## Chapter 6: Sustainable Living

In the face of escalating environmental challenges, sustainable living has emerged as a crucial approach to preserving our planet for future generations. Sustainability involves making choices that meet our present needs without compromising the ability of future generations to meet theirs. It encompasses a wide range of practices, from reducing waste to conserving resources and promoting environmental stewardship. By adopting a sustainable lifestyle, we contribute to the health of our planet and ensure a better quality of life for ourselves and future generations.

The importance of sustainability cannot be overstated. Our planet's resources are finite, and the impact of human activity on the environment has reached alarming levels. Climate change, deforestation, pollution, and the depletion of natural resources are just a few of the pressing issues we face. Sustainable living addresses these challenges by promoting practices that reduce our ecological footprint and foster a harmonious relationship with nature.

Simplicity and frugality are closely intertwined with sustainability. By embracing a simpler lifestyle, we naturally consume less and waste less, leading to a lower environmental impact. Frugality encourages us to be mindful of our resources, making thoughtful decisions that prioritize long-term well-being over short-term gratification. Together, simplicity and frugality form the foundation of sustainable living, enabling us to live in a way that respects and preserves the natural world.

One inspiring advocate for sustainable living is Vandana Shiva, an Indian scholar, environmental activist, and food sovereignty advocate. Shiva's work emphasizes the interconnectedness of human and ecological well-being. She has dedicated her life to promoting sustainable agriculture, biodiversity, and the rights of indigenous communities.

Vandana Shiva's journey began with a deep connection to nature and a desire to protect it. She founded the Research Foundation for Science, Technology, and Ecology in 1982, focusing on sustainable agricultural practices and the preservation of biodiversity. Shiva's advocacy extends to challenging the industrial agricultural system, which she believes contributes to environmental degradation, loss of biodiversity, and social injustice.

Shiva's philosophy of sustainable living is rooted in the principles of ecological harmony and social justice. She champions the idea that small-scale, local farming practices are essential for environmental sustainability and community well-being. Through her work with Navdanya, a movement she founded to promote biodiversity conservation and organic farming, Shiva has empowered countless farmers to adopt sustainable practices that restore soil health, conserve water, and protect seeds.

One of Shiva's notable contributions is her advocacy for seed sovereignty—the right of farmers to save, use, exchange, and sell their own seeds. She argues that corporate control over seeds threatens biodiversity and the livelihoods of small farmers. By promoting seed diversity and traditional farming methods, Shiva aims to create a more resilient and sustainable food system.

Vandana Shiva's efforts highlight the profound impact that individual and collective actions can have on the environment. Her work inspires us to rethink our relationship with nature and to adopt practices that promote sustainability and social equity. By following her example, we can make meaningful contributions to the health of our planet and the well-being of our communities.

Adopting sustainable living practices involves making conscious choices that reduce our environmental impact. Here are some practical tips to help you embrace sustainability in your daily life:

1. Reduce, Reuse, Recycle: This classic mantra of sustainability is a powerful starting point. Reduce your consumption by choosing products with minimal packaging and opting for reusable items instead of disposable ones. Reuse items whenever

possible and recycle materials to give them a second life.

2. Conserve Energy: Reducing energy consumption is a key aspect of sustainable living. Turn off lights and appliances when not in use, use energy-efficient bulbs, and consider investing in renewable energy sources like solar panels. Simple actions, such as unplugging chargers and setting thermostats to energy-saving temperatures, can make a significant difference.

3. Save Water: Water is a precious resource that should be used wisely. Fix any leaks in your home, take shorter showers, and install water-efficient fixtures. Collect rainwater for gardening and use native plants that require less water. Being mindful of water usage helps conserve this vital resource.

4. Choose Sustainable Transportation: Transportation is a major contributor to carbon emissions. Whenever possible, opt for walking, biking, or using public transportation. If you drive, consider carpooling or using an electric or fuel-efficient vehicle. Reducing your reliance on fossil fuels can significantly lower your carbon footprint.

5. Support Sustainable Agriculture: Choose organic and locally-produced foods that are grown using sustainable practices. Supporting farmers who use environmentally-friendly methods helps reduce the environmental impact of agriculture and promotes biodiversity. Additionally, consider growing your

own food through gardening or participating in community-supported agriculture (CSA) programs.

6. Reduce Meat Consumption: The production of meat has a significant environmental impact, contributing to deforestation, water consumption, and greenhouse gas emissions. Reducing your meat intake and opting for plant-based meals can lower your ecological footprint and improve your health.

7. Minimize Waste: Aim to produce as little waste as possible. Compost organic waste to create nutrient-rich soil for your garden. Avoid single-use plastics and choose products with minimal packaging. By minimizing waste, you contribute to a cleaner environment and reduce the burden on landfills.

8. Choose Eco-Friendly Products: When making purchases, look for products that are environmentally friendly and sustainably sourced. This includes items made from recycled materials, biodegradable products, and those that have been certified by environmental organizations. Supporting eco-friendly brands encourages more sustainable practices in the market.

9. Educate Yourself and Others: Stay informed about environmental issues and sustainable practices. Share your knowledge with others and encourage your community to adopt sustainable habits. Collective action can drive significant change and create a more sustainable world.

10. Advocate for Change: Use your voice to advocate for environmental policies and practices. Support organizations and initiatives that promote sustainability and participate in local efforts to protect the environment. By advocating for change, you can help create a more sustainable future for all.

Embracing sustainable living is a journey that requires ongoing effort and commitment. It involves making mindful choices in every aspect of our lives, from the products we buy to the way we use resources. By integrating sustainability into our daily routines, we can make a positive impact on the environment and contribute to the well-being of future generations.

Vandana Shiva's advocacy for sustainable living serves as a powerful reminder of the interconnectedness of human and ecological health. Her work inspires us to consider the broader implications of our actions and to strive for a more just and sustainable world. By following her example, we can adopt practices that protect our planet and promote the health and happiness of all its inhabitants.

In our exploration of simple and frugal living, we find that sustainability is a key component. By living sustainably, we align our actions with our values and contribute to the greater good. Each small step towards sustainability brings us closer to a healthier planet and a more fulfilling life.

Sustainable living is essential for preserving our planet and ensuring a better future for generations to come. By understanding the importance of sustainability and how simplicity and frugality contribute to it, we can make informed choices that reduce our environmental impact. The story of Vandana Shiva highlights the power of individual and collective action in promoting sustainability and social justice.

Adopting sustainable living practices requires a commitment to mindfulness and intentionality. By following the practical tips outlined in this chapter, you can integrate sustainability into your daily life and make a positive difference. Remember that each small step counts, and collectively, our actions can lead to significant change.

As you continue your journey towards a simpler and more sustainable life, stay inspired by the examples of those who have dedicated their lives to environmental stewardship. Let their stories motivate you to act and embrace a lifestyle that respects and preserves the natural world.

The journey to sustainable living is ongoing, but the rewards are immense. By living in harmony with nature, we can create a healthier, more just, and more beautiful world. Embrace the principles of simplicity, frugality, and sustainability, and discover the joy and fulfilment that come from living a life aligned with your values.

## Chapter 7: Finding Happiness in Simplicity

In our relentless pursuit of happiness, we often find ourselves entangled in the complexities of modern life—chasing after material possessions, social status, and a never-ending to-do list. Yet, amid this chaos, there lies a timeless truth: happiness can often be found in the simplicity of life. By stripping away the nonessential and focusing on what truly matters, we can uncover a profound sense of joy and fulfilment that transcends the superficial allure of material wealth.

The connection between simplicity and happiness is deeply rooted in the idea that less is more. When we simplify our lives, we remove the distractions that prevent us from appreciating the present moment. We create space for meaningful experiences, relationships, and personal growth. Simplicity invites us to live with intention, aligning our actions with our values and priorities. It allows us to focus on what truly brings us joy, rather than what society dictates we should pursue.

Psychologically, simple living offers numerous benefits. It reduces stress and anxiety by eliminating the overwhelming clutter—both physical and mental—that can weigh us down. A simpler life fosters a sense of control and agency, as we make conscious choices about how we spend our time and resources. This intentionality can lead to greater satisfaction and a deeper connection to our inner selves.

Research supports the psychological benefits of simplicity. Studies have shown that individuals who embrace minimalist lifestyles report higher levels of well-being and life satisfaction. By prioritizing experiences over possessions and focusing on quality over quantity, they cultivate a sense of contentment that is resilient to external circumstances. The practice of mindfulness, often associated with simple living, further enhances this well-being by grounding us in the present and helping us appreciate the beauty of everyday moments.

One individual who has masterfully harnessed the power of simplicity to find happiness is Leo Babauta, the creator of the popular blog Zen Habits. Babauta's journey toward simplicity began out of necessity—he was overwhelmed by his chaotic life, struggling with debt, unhealthy habits, and the pressures of modern living. Determined to make a change, he embarked on a transformative journey of decluttering and mindfulness.

Leo Babauta started small, focusing on one habit at a time. He began by decluttering his physical space, letting go of items that no longer served a purpose or brought joy. This initial step had a cascading effect, leading him to simplify other areas of his life, from his daily routines to his relationships.

Babauta found that by reducing the noise and distractions, he could focus more on what truly mattered to him.

Zen Habits, the blog he created to document his journey, quickly gained a following. People from all walks of life resonated with his message of simplicity and intentional living. Babauta's writing emphasized the importance of mindfulness, the power of small changes, and the joy of living with less. His approach was practical and compassionate, encouraging readers to find their own path to simplicity.

One of the key principles that Babauta advocates is the idea of "single-tasking." In a world that glorifies multitasking, he discovered that focusing on one task at a time not only improved his productivity but also his overall well-being. By giving his full attention to the present moment, he was able to engage more deeply with his work and find satisfaction in the process.

Babauta's journey with Zen Habits serves as a powerful reminder that simplicity is not about deprivation but about liberation. It is about freeing ourselves from the unnecessary burdens that prevent us from living fully and authentically. Through his experiences, we see that happiness is not something to be chased but something to be cultivated through mindful and intentional living.

To embark on your own journey towards finding happiness in simplicity, consider these practical tips:

1. Prioritize Your Values: Begin by identifying what truly matters to you. Reflect on your core values and what brings you genuine joy. Use these insights to guide your decisions and actions, ensuring that your life aligns with your deepest aspirations.

2. Declutter Your Environment: Start with your physical space. Remove items that no longer serve a purpose or bring you joy. Creating an organized, clutter-free environment can have a profound impact on your mental clarity and emotional well-being.

3. Embrace Mindfulness: Incorporate mindfulness practices into your daily routine. Whether through meditation, deep breathing, or simply paying attention to the present moment, mindfulness can help you appreciate the beauty of simplicity and find joy in everyday experiences.

4. Simplify Your Schedule: Evaluate your commitments and identify areas where you can simplify. Focus on activities that align with your values and bring you happiness. Learn to say no to obligations that do not contribute to your well-being.

5. Nurture Meaningful Relationships: Invest time and energy in building and nurturing relationships that bring joy and fulfilment. Surround yourself with people who uplift and support you and let go of toxic relationships that drain your energy.

6. Practice Gratitude: Cultivate a sense of gratitude by regularly reflecting on the positive aspects of your life. Keep a gratitude journal and write down things you are thankful for each day. This practice can shift your focus from what you lack to what you have, fostering a sense of contentment.

7. Limit Digital Distractions: In today's digital age, it's easy to become overwhelmed by screens and constant connectivity. Set boundaries for your use of technology and make time for offline activities that bring you joy, such as reading, spending time in nature, or engaging in hobbies.

8. Focus on Experiences Over Possessions: Prioritize experiences and relationships over material possessions. Spend your time and money on activities that create lasting memories and bring you joy. This shift in focus can lead to a more fulfilling and meaningful life.

9. Adopt a Minimalist Mindset: Embrace minimalism by focusing on quality over quantity. Choose possessions, activities, and relationships that add value to your life and let go of anything

that doesn't. Minimalism can help you create a life that is rich in meaning and joy.

10. Create a Daily Routine: Establishing a simple and consistent daily routine can help you stay organized and focused. Prioritize your most important tasks and set aside time for self-care and relaxation. A well-structured routine can reduce stress and increase productivity.

Incorporating these practices into your life, you may find that simplicity becomes a source of profound happiness. By focusing on what truly matters and letting go of the unnecessary, you create space for joy, peace, and fulfilment.

The journey to finding happiness in simplicity is unique for each individual. It requires patience, self-compassion, and a willingness to let go of societal expectations. But as Leo Babauta's story illustrates, the rewards are immense. Through mindful and intentional living, you can uncover a deep sense of joy and contentment that transcends the superficial allure of material wealth.

Simplicity also fosters resilience and adaptability. When we are not burdened by excess, we can navigate life's challenges with greater ease and grace. The clarity and focus that come with simplicity enable us to respond to difficulties with a calm and centred mind. This resilience not only enhances our well-being but also empowers us to support others and contribute positively to our communities.

Moreover, simplicity encourages us to live in harmony with the natural world. By reducing our consumption and making mindful choices, we can lessen our environmental impact and promote sustainability. This alignment with nature brings a sense of interconnectedness and responsibility, deepening our appreciation for the beauty and abundance of the Earth.

The psychological benefits of simplicity extend to our relationships as well. When we prioritize meaningful connections over material possessions, we create deeper and more fulfilling bonds with others. Simplicity encourages us to be present and engaged, fostering empathy, understanding, and mutual support. These rich, authentic relationships become a source of lasting happiness and fulfilment.

While exploring the principles of simple living in this book, remember that the journey is ongoing. There is no final destination, no perfect state of simplicity. Instead, it is a continuous process of self-discovery and intentionality. Each step you take towards simplicity brings you closer to a life of greater happiness and fulfilment. Together, we will uncover the beauty and fulfilment that come from living a life of intentional simplicity.

Reflect on the words of the ancient Chinese philosopher Laozi: "Simplicity, patience, compassion. These three are your greatest treasures." Embrace these treasures as you journey towards a simpler, more joyful life. By cultivating simplicity, you can unlock the profound happiness that lies within and create a life that is rich in meaning, purpose, and joy.

## Chapter 8: Mindful Consumption

In this world where consumerism often dictates our choices and behaviours, the concept of mindful consumption offers a refreshing and necessary counterbalance. Mindful consumption is the practice of making intentional, thoughtful decisions about what we buy and how we use resources. It involves being fully aware of the impact of our consumption habits on our well-being, the environment, and society at large.

At its core, mindful consumption is about aligning our purchases and lifestyle choices with our values and priorities. It challenges us to consider the true cost of our consumption—not just in terms of money, but also in terms of environmental degradation, social justice, and personal satisfaction. By embracing mindful consumption, we can reduce waste, support ethical businesses, and create a more sustainable and fulfilling life.

Practising mindful consumption begins with awareness. It requires us to be conscious of our buying habits and to question whether our purchases are truly necessary and meaningful. This mindfulness extends beyond the act of buying to how we use, maintain, and dispose of our possessions. It encourages us to appreciate what we have, rather than constantly seeking more.

An inspiring example of mindful consumption in action is the story of Yvon Chouinard, the founder of Patagonia, an outdoor clothing and gear company known for its commitment to environmental sustainability and ethical business practices. Chouinard's philosophy of mindful consumption is deeply embedded in Patagonia's corporate culture and operations.

Yvon Chouinard's journey began with a passion for climbing and a desire to create high-quality, durable gear that would have minimal environmental impact. From the outset, he was determined to build a company that would not only provide excellent products but also uphold strong environmental and social values. Under his leadership, Patagonia has become a pioneer in sustainable business practices.

Patagonia's approach to mindful consumption is multifaceted. The company emphasizes the importance of making products that are built to last, reducing the need for frequent replacements. They use environmentally friendly materials and processes, such as organic cotton and recycled fabrics, to minimize their ecological footprint. Patagonia also encourages customers to repair and reuse their products through initiatives like the Worn Wear program, which promotes the longevity of their gear.

One of Patagonia's most notable campaigns is the "Don't Buy This Jacket" advertisement, which ran in The New York Times on Black Friday in 2011. The ad featured a Patagonia jacket and urged consumers to consider the environmental impact of their purchases and to buy only what they truly needed. This bold move underscored the company's commitment to mindful consumption and challenged the prevailing culture of overconsumption.

Chouinard's vision for Patagonia extends beyond product sustainability. The company is also dedicated to social responsibility, advocating for fair labour practices and supporting grassroots environmental organizations. Patagonia donates a portion of its profits to environmental causes and actively engages in campaigns to protect natural habitats and combat climate change.

The story of Yvon Chouinard and Patagonia serves as a powerful example of how businesses can thrive by embracing mindful consumption and sustainability. It demonstrates that profitability and ethical responsibility are not mutually exclusive but can complement and enhance each other.

To incorporate mindful consumption into your own life, consider the following practical tips:

1. Reflect on Your Needs: Before making a purchase, take a moment to reflect on whether the item is truly necessary. Ask yourself if it aligns with

your values and if it will genuinely enhance your life. Avoid impulse buys by creating a waiting period before making non-essential purchases.

2. Choose Quality Over Quantity: Invest in high-quality, durable items that will last longer and serve you better. While these products may have a higher upfront cost, they can save you money in the long run by reducing the need for frequent replacements.

3. Support Ethical Brands: Do your research and support companies that prioritize sustainability, fair labour practices, and environmental responsibility. Look for certifications like Fair Trade, B Corp, and organic labels that indicate a commitment to ethical standards.

4. Reduce Waste: Be mindful of the waste generated by your consumption habits. Opt for products with minimal packaging, reusable items, and bulk purchases to reduce single-use plastics. Compost organic waste and recycle whenever possible.

5. Repair and Reuse: Extend the life of your possessions by repairing them when they break or wear out. Learn basic repair skills or take advantage of repair services. Repurpose items creatively to give them a new life and avoid unnecessary waste.

6. Embrace Minimalism: Adopting a minimalist mindset can help you focus on what truly matters and reduce unnecessary consumption. Simplify your

belongings and keep only those items that bring you joy and serve a purpose. This approach can lead to a more organized and fulfilling life.

7. Be Mindful of Energy Use: Consider the energy consumption of the products you buy and use. Opt for energy-efficient appliances and electronics and be conscious of your overall energy use. Simple actions like turning off lights when not in use and unplugging devices can make a significant difference.

8. Buy Local: Support local businesses and artisans who produce goods sustainably and ethically. Buying local reduces the carbon footprint associated with transportation and helps strengthen your community's economy.

9. Educate Yourself: Stay informed about the environmental and social impacts of consumer goods. Read labels, research companies, and seek out resources that provide information on sustainable and ethical consumption.

10. Advocate for Change: Use your voice to advocate for policies and practices that promote mindful consumption and sustainability. Support initiatives that aim to reduce waste, protect the environment, and ensure fair labour practices. Collective action can drive significant change and create a more sustainable future.

Practicing mindful consumption is a journey that requires continuous reflection and adjustment. It involves making conscious choices that align with your values and recognizing the broader impact of your actions. By adopting mindful consumption habits, you can contribute to a more sustainable and equitable world while enhancing your own well-being.

Incorporating mindfulness into your consumption habits can also lead to a deeper appreciation for the things you own. When we take the time to carefully consider our purchases and choose items that truly resonate with us, we develop a stronger connection to our belongings. This connection fosters a sense of gratitude and contentment, reducing the desire for constant acquisition and allowing us to focus on the richness of our existing resources.

Yvon Chouinard's philosophy and Patagonia's practices exemplify the powerful impact that mindful consumption can have, not just on individuals, but on communities and the planet as a whole. Their commitment to sustainability and ethical business practices serves as an inspiring model for how we can integrate these principles into our own lives.

One of the most significant aspects of mindful consumption is its ability to foster a sense of responsibility and stewardship. By being mindful of our consumption choices, we acknowledge our role in the larger ecological and social systems. This awareness can inspire us to take actions that support the well-being of the planet and its inhabitants, from reducing our carbon footprint to supporting fair labour practices.

As we navigate the complexities of modern life, mindful consumption offers a pathway to greater harmony and balance. It challenges us to rethink our relationship with material goods and to prioritize values such as sustainability, ethical responsibility, and personal fulfilment. By making mindful choices, we can create a more intentional and meaningful life.

The journey towards mindful consumption is ongoing and ever-evolving. It requires us to be vigilant and intentional in our daily choices, constantly seeking ways to reduce our impact and live more sustainably. However, the rewards of this journey are immense, offering not only personal satisfaction but also a profound sense of connection to the world around us.

Mindful consumption is a powerful practice that can transform our lives and the world we live in. By being intentional about our buying habits and considering the broader impact of our consumption, we can contribute to a more sustainable and equitable future. The story of Yvon Chouinard and Patagonia exemplifies how businesses and individuals alike can thrive by embracing principles of mindful consumption.

As you incorporate these practices into your own life, remember that every small step counts. Whether it's choosing to buy less, supporting ethical brands, or reducing waste, each mindful decision helps create a ripple effect that can lead to significant positive change.

Let the journey of mindful consumption be one of continuous learning and growth. Stay curious, stay informed, and remain committed to making choices that align with your values. By doing so, you can cultivate a life that is not only fulfilling and meaningful but also contributes to the well-being of the planet and its people.

As we move forward in this exploration of simple and frugal living, continue to reflect on how these principles intersect with your daily life. Each chapter of this book offers insights and practical tips to help you simplify your life and find happiness in the everyday moments. Together, we will uncover the beauty and fulfilment that come from living a life of intentional simplicity and mindful consumption.

## Chapter 9: Simple and Healthy Eating

In a world where fast food chains and processed meals dominate the landscape, the art of simple and healthy eating offers a refreshing return to the basics. The benefits of a simple diet extend far beyond physical health; they encompass mental clarity, emotional well-being, and even environmental sustainability. By focusing on whole, unprocessed foods and mindful eating practices, we can nourish our bodies and souls while cultivating a deeper connection to the food we consume.

The journey towards simple and healthy eating begins with understanding the benefits of a simple diet. At its core, a simple diet emphasizes natural, minimally processed foods that are rich in nutrients. This approach to eating is not about deprivation or restriction but about choosing foods that fuel our bodies and minds in the most natural way possible.

One of the primary benefits of a simple diet is improved health. Whole foods—such as fruits, vegetables, whole grains, nuts, seeds, and lean proteins—are packed with essential vitamins, minerals, and antioxidants that support our overall well-being. These nutrients help boost our immune system, reduce inflammation, and lower the risk of chronic diseases such as heart disease, diabetes, and cancer. By eliminating processed foods and artificial additives, we can also reduce the burden on our digestive system and promote better gut health.

A significant advantage of a simple diet is increased energy levels. Processed foods, with their high sugar and unhealthy fat content, often lead to energy crashes and fatigue. In contrast, whole foods provide a steady release of energy, keeping us feeling more vibrant and alert throughout the day. This sustained energy allows us to be more productive, focused, and engaged in our daily activities.

Simple and healthy eating also has profound psychological benefits. The act of preparing and consuming wholesome foods can be a meditative practice, fostering mindfulness and a sense of gratitude. When we take the time to cook and enjoy our meals, we become more attuned to our body's needs and hunger cues, leading to better portion control and a healthier relationship with food. This mindful approach to eating can help reduce stress, anxiety, and emotional eating.

Frugal and nutritious meal planning is an essential component of simple and healthy eating. Contrary to popular belief, eating well does not have to be expensive. With thoughtful planning and smart shopping, it is possible to create delicious, nutrient-dense meals on a budget.

One of the pioneers of the simple eating movement is Michael Pollan, an acclaimed author and food advocate whose philosophy has influenced countless individuals to rethink their relationship with food. Pollan's mantra, "Eat food, not too much, mostly plants," encapsulates the essence of a simple and healthy diet.

Michael Pollan's journey began with a curiosity about the origins of the food on his plate. His exploration led him to uncover the often troubling realities of industrial agriculture and food production. Through his books, such as "The Omnivore's Dilemma" and "In Defense of Food," Pollan advocates for a return to traditional food practices that prioritize health, sustainability, and simplicity.

Pollan emphasizes the importance of eating real food—foods that are as close to their natural state as possible. He encourages consumers to avoid products with long ingredient lists, especially those containing additives and preservatives. Instead, he advocates for whole foods that our ancestors would recognize as food.

In addition to promoting whole foods, Pollan highlights the benefits of plant-based eating. While not advocating for strict vegetarianism, he suggests that the majority of our diet should consist of fruits, vegetables, legumes, nuts, and seeds. These plant-based foods are not only nutritious but also have a lower environmental impact compared to animal products.

Pollan's philosophy also extends to mindful eating practices. He encourages individuals to take the time to savour their meals, eat at a table rather than on the go, and enjoy the communal aspects of dining. By making eating a deliberate and pleasurable activity, we can foster a healthier relationship with food and cultivate a greater appreciation for the nourishment it provides.

To incorporate the principles of simple and healthy eating into your life, consider these practical tips for frugal and nutritious meal planning:

1. Plan Your Meals: Start by creating a weekly meal plan that includes breakfast, lunch, dinner, and snacks. Planning your meals in advance helps you stay organized, reduce food waste, and avoid last-minute unhealthy choices. Choose recipes that are simple, nutritious, and use seasonal ingredients.

2. Shop Smart: Make a shopping list based on your meal plan and stick to it. Buy in bulk for staples like grains, beans, and nuts, which can save money in the long run. Shop at farmers' markets or join a community-supported agriculture (CSA) program to access fresh, locally-grown produce at lower prices.

3. Cook at Home: Preparing meals at home gives you control over the ingredients and cooking methods, ensuring that your meals are healthier and more affordable. Batch cooking and meal prepping can save time and make it easier to stick to your healthy eating goals.

4. Embrace Plant-Based Meals: Incorporate more plant-based meals into your diet. Beans, lentils, and tofu are cost-effective sources of protein that can be used in a variety of dishes. Experiment with vegetarian and vegan recipes to discover new flavours and textures.

5. Utilize Leftovers: Don't let leftovers go to waste. Repurpose them into new meals, such as turning roasted vegetables into a hearty soup or using leftover grains in a stir-fry. This not only saves money but also reduces food waste.

6. Grow Your Own Food: If you have the space, consider starting a small garden. Growing your own herbs, vegetables, and fruits can be a rewarding and cost-effective way to access fresh, organic produce. Even a few potted plants on a balcony can make a difference.

7. Simplify Your Ingredients: Focus on recipes that use a few simple, whole ingredients. Avoid complex dishes that require numerous speciality items. Simple recipes are often more nutritious and easier to prepare.

8. Snack Wisely: Choose healthy snacks like fresh fruit, nuts, seeds, and yoghurt instead of processed snacks high in sugar and unhealthy fats. Preparing your snacks in advance can help you avoid reaching for unhealthy options when hunger strikes.

9. Stay Hydrated: Drinking plenty of water is essential for overall health. Keep a reusable water bottle with you to stay hydrated throughout the day. Herbal teas and infused water with fruits and herbs can also be a refreshing and healthy alternative to sugary drinks.

10. Practice Mindful Eating: Take the time to enjoy your meals without distractions. Eat slowly, savour each bite, and listen to your body's hunger and fullness cues. Mindful eating can enhance your enjoyment of food and prevent overeating.

Embracing a simple and healthy diet is not just about what we eat but how we eat. By making deliberate, thoughtful choices, we can transform our relationship with food and create a more nourishing, fulfilling life. Michael Pollan's food philosophy reminds us that eating well is within our reach and that simplicity is key to both health and happiness.

Let the principles of simple and healthy eating guide you towards a more intentional and mindful approach to nourishment. The journey towards better eating habits is a personal one, and there is no one-size-fits-all solution. Experiment with different foods, recipes, and practices to discover what works best for you and your lifestyle.

The benefits of a simple diet are vast and far-reaching. From improved physical health to enhanced mental clarity and emotional well-being, eating simple and wholesome foods can transform our lives. By adopting frugal and nutritious meal-planning strategies, we can make healthy eating accessible and sustainable.

The story of Michael Pollan and his food philosophy serves as an inspiration for us all. His advocacy for whole foods, plant-based eating, and mindful consumption highlights the profound impact that our food choices can have on our health and the environment. Pollan's approach encourages us to reconnect with the natural rhythms of eating and to find joy in the simplicity of nourishing our bodies.

On your journey towards simple and healthy eating, think that small changes can lead to significant results. Start by incorporating a few of these practical tips into your daily routine and gradually build on them. The path to better health and well-being is a continuous process, and every step you take brings you closer to a more balanced and fulfilling life.

Embrace the beauty of simple and healthy eating, and let it be a cornerstone of your journey towards a simpler, more intentional life. As you savour the flavours and nourishment of wholesome foods, you will discover the joy and satisfaction that come from living in harmony with nature and honouring your body's needs.

## Chapter 10: Building Meaningful Relationships

In the realm of simple living, relationships play a pivotal role. They provide emotional support, enhance our sense of belonging, and contribute significantly to our overall well-being. Building and nurturing meaningful relationships is essential for a fulfilling life, as it is through these connections that we experience love, joy, and a sense of community. The essence of simple living is not just about reducing physical clutter but also about fostering deep, meaningful connections with others.

The importance of relationships in simple living cannot be overstated. Human beings are inherently social creatures, and our happiness is closely tied to the quality of our relationships. Research consistently shows that strong social connections are linked to better mental and physical health, increased longevity, and greater life satisfaction. By prioritizing relationships, we can create a supportive network that helps us navigate the challenges of life and celebrate its joys.

Nurturing relationships without materialism involves focusing on the emotional and spiritual aspects of our connections rather than material wealth or status. In a society that often equates success with material possessions, it is easy to fall into the trap of believing that gifts and luxuries are the keys to building strong relationships. However, the most meaningful connections are built on mutual respect, understanding, and shared experiences.

One of the most profound teachers of compassion and meaningful relationships is the Dalai Lama. His teachings emphasize the importance of empathy, kindness, and compassion in building strong, loving connections with others. The Dalai Lama's philosophy is rooted in the belief that all beings are interconnected, and that true happiness comes from nurturing these connections with an open heart.

The Dalai Lama often speaks about the value of compassion as the foundation of all meaningful relationships. He teaches that by cultivating a compassionate mindset, we can overcome the barriers that separate us from others and build deeper, more authentic connections. Compassion involves understanding and empathizing with the experiences and emotions of others, offering support and kindness without expecting anything in return.

One of the Dalai Lama's key teachings is the idea that genuine happiness comes from focusing on the well-being of others. He believes that when we prioritize the happiness and well-being of those around us, we not only strengthen our relationships but also find greater fulfilment in our own lives. This selfless approach to relationships fosters a sense of unity and interconnectedness that transcends materialism.

To cultivate meaningful relationships, we can draw inspiration from the Dalai Lama's teachings and incorporate practical strategies into our daily lives. Here are some tips to help you build and nurture relationships without relying on materialism:

1. Practice Active Listening: One of the most powerful ways to connect with others is by truly listening to them. Give your full attention during conversations, avoid interrupting, and show empathy towards their feelings and experiences. Active listening demonstrates respect and helps build trust.

2. Show Appreciation: Regularly express gratitude and appreciation for the people in your life. Acknowledge their efforts, celebrate their achievements, and let them know how much they mean to you. Small gestures of appreciation can go a long way in strengthening relationships.

3. Spend Quality Time Together: Prioritize spending quality time with your loved ones. Engage in activities that you both enjoy, whether it's cooking a meal together, going for a walk, or simply having a heartfelt conversation. Quality time fosters deeper connections and creates lasting memories.

4. Be Present: In our fast-paced world, it's easy to become distracted by technology and other demands. Make a conscious effort to be present

when you're with others. Put away your phone, focus on the moment, and engage fully with the people around you.

5. Offer Support: Be there for your friends and family during both good times and challenging moments. Offer your support, lend a helping hand, and provide a shoulder to lean on. Being reliable and supportive strengthens the bonds of trust and loyalty.

6. Practice Empathy: Strive to understand and empathize with the feelings and perspectives of others. Put yourself in their shoes and consider how they might be experiencing a situation. Empathy fosters compassion and helps you build deeper, more meaningful connections.

7. Communicate Openly: Honest and open communication is the cornerstone of any healthy relationship. Share your thoughts, feelings, and concerns with your loved ones, and encourage them to do the same. Open communication helps prevent misunderstandings and strengthens mutual understanding.

8. Respect Differences: Embrace the diversity of thoughts, beliefs, and experiences that each person brings to a relationship. Respecting differences fosters a sense of acceptance and inclusion, allowing relationships to flourish in an atmosphere of mutual respect.

9. Engage in Shared Activities: Find common interests and engage in activities that you can enjoy together. Whether it's a hobby, a sport, or a volunteer project, shared activities provide opportunities to bond and create meaningful experiences.

10. Practice Forgiveness: No relationship is without its challenges. When conflicts arise, practice forgiveness and work towards resolving issues with a compassionate heart. Holding onto grudges can harm relationships, while forgiveness fosters healing and growth.

The Dalai Lama's teachings remind us that the foundation of meaningful relationships lies in compassion, empathy, and selflessness. By focusing on these principles, we can build connections that are rich in love and understanding, free from the constraints of materialism.

Building meaningful relationships also involves creating a supportive community. Surround yourself with people who uplift and inspire you and be that source of support for others. A strong community provides a sense of belonging and connection, enriching our lives and contributing to our overall well-being.

The journey to nurturing meaningful relationships is an ongoing process that requires intention, effort, and a genuine desire to connect with others. It is about cultivating a mindset of compassion, empathy, and selflessness, and letting go of the need for material validation. As we embrace these principles, we create a ripple effect that extends beyond our immediate relationships, fostering a more compassionate and connected world.

In conclusion, building meaningful relationships is a vital aspect of simple living. The Dalai Lama's teachings on compassion and empathy provide valuable insights into how we can cultivate deep, authentic connections with others. By practicing active listening, showing appreciation, spending quality time together, and being present, we can strengthen our relationships and create a supportive community.

Relationships are the heart of a fulfilling life. Nurture them with care, compassion, and genuine effort. The connections you build will not only enrich your own life but also bring joy and support to those around you.

Let the principles of compassion and empathy guide you in your interactions with others. Embrace the beauty of meaningful relationships and discover the profound happiness that comes from connecting with others on a deep, authentic level. Together, we can create a world that values and prioritizes the well-being of all its inhabitants.

## Chapter 11: Embracing Nature

In our fast-paced, technology-driven world, the importance of connecting with nature is often overlooked. Yet, nature plays a crucial role in a simple and fulfilling life. Embracing nature allows us to slow down, appreciate the beauty around us, and find peace in the simplicity of the natural world. The benefits of connecting with nature are vast, impacting our physical health, mental well-being, and overall quality of life.

The role of nature in a simple life is multifaceted. It provides a sanctuary from the constant noise and stress of modern living, offering a space where we can reconnect with ourselves and the world around us. Nature encourages us to live more mindfully, paying attention to the present moment and the intricate details of our environment. This mindfulness fosters a sense of wonder and gratitude, enhancing our overall well-being.

Connecting with nature also has numerous physical health benefits. Spending time outdoors has been shown to boost our immune system, reduce blood pressure, and improve cardiovascular health. Exposure to natural sunlight helps regulate our sleep-wake cycles, improving sleep quality and overall energy levels. Additionally, engaging in outdoor activities such as hiking, gardening, or simply walking in a park provides physical exercise, contributing to better fitness and health.

The mental health benefits of nature are equally significant. Nature has a calming effect on the mind, reducing stress, anxiety, and depression. Studies have shown that spending time in natural settings can improve mood, enhance cognitive function, and increase feelings of happiness and well-being. Nature's ability to soothe the mind and lift the spirit makes it an essential component of a balanced and fulfilling life.

One of the most passionate advocates for the power of nature was John Muir, a naturalist, author, and early environmentalist whose love for the wilderness inspired a movement to protect America's natural landscapes. Muir's profound connection to nature and his eloquent writings about its beauty and importance have left a lasting legacy that continues to inspire people to this day.

John Muir's love for nature began in his childhood when he spent countless hours exploring the woods and fields near his home in Dunbar, Scotland. Born on April 21, 1838, Muir's early life was steeped in the natural beauty of the Scottish countryside, which left an indelible mark on his soul. His family emigrated to the United States in 1849, settling in Wisconsin. There, Muir's passion for the natural world continued to flourish as he explored the American wilderness.

Muir's formal education was intermittent, as he was often required to work on the family farm. However, his innate curiosity and love for learning drove him to study nature on his own. He attended the University of Wisconsin for a few years, where he studied subjects like botany, geology, and chemistry, which deepened his understanding and appreciation of the natural world.

A turning point in Muir's life came in 1867 when he suffered a debilitating eye injury while working in a factory. This event prompted him to reassess his life's direction. Once he recovered, Muir embarked on a transformative journey, walking from Indiana to Florida, a trek of over a thousand miles. This journey, chronicled in his book "A Thousand-Mile Walk to the Gulf," marked the beginning of Muir's lifelong dedication to exploring and preserving nature.

In 1868, Muir arrived in California and discovered the Yosemite Valley, a place that would become central to his life's work. He spent years exploring the Sierra Nevada mountains, studying their geology, and documenting their natural beauty.

Muir's writings about Yosemite captivated readers and brought national attention to the need for its preservation.

Muir's eloquent and passionate writings played a crucial role in the establishment of Yosemite National Park in 1890. His essays and books, filled with vivid descriptions of nature's wonders, inspired a generation of Americans to appreciate and protect their natural heritage. Muir's ability to convey the spiritual and transcendent qualities of nature helped foster a growing conservation movement in the United States.

One of John Muir's most significant contributions was his role in the founding of the Sierra Club in 1892. The Sierra Club, one of the first large-scale environmental preservation organizations in the United States, aimed to protect and preserve the natural beauty of the Sierra Nevada and other wild places. Muir served as the club's first president and used his influence to advocate for the conservation of wilderness areas.

Muir's advocacy extended beyond Yosemite. He campaigned for the creation of several other national parks, including Sequoia, Mount Rainier, Petrified Forest, and Grand Canyon National Parks. His efforts were instrumental in expanding the national park system and ensuring that future generations could experience the unspoiled beauty of America's natural landscapes.

Throughout his life, Muir maintained a deep spiritual connection to nature. He saw the natural world as a reflection of the divine and believed that spending time in nature was essential for the soul's nourishment. His philosophy of nature as a source of spiritual renewal is evident in his writings, which often describe his experiences in the wilderness as profound and transformative.

One of Muir's most famous quotes, "The mountains are calling, and I must go," encapsulates his enduring love for the wilderness and his belief in the healing power of nature. Muir's legacy continues to inspire environmentalists, hikers, and nature lovers around the world. His vision of preserving the natural world for future generations remains a guiding principle for the modern conservation movement.

To embrace nature in your own life, check these practical tips for connecting with the natural world:

1. Spend Time Outdoors: Make a conscious effort to spend more time outside. Whether it's a daily walk in the park, a weekend hike, or a camping trip, immersing yourself in nature can have a rejuvenating effect on your mind and body.

2. Create a Green Space: If you have limited access to natural areas, create your own green space at home. Plant a garden, set up a few potted plants, or create a small indoor herb garden. Bringing nature

into your living space can provide many of the same benefits as spending time outdoors.

3. Practice Mindfulness in Nature: When you're in a natural setting, practice mindfulness by paying attention to the sights, sounds, and smells around you. Notice the rustling leaves, the chirping birds, and the fresh scent of the earth. This mindfulness can deepen your connection to nature and enhance your sense of well-being.

4. Engage in Outdoor Activities: Find activities that allow you to enjoy nature while also providing physical exercise. Hiking, biking, kayaking, and gardening are all great ways to stay active and connect with the natural world.

5. Learn About Local Wildlife: Take the time to learn about the plants and animals that inhabit your local area. Understanding the ecosystems around you can deepen your appreciation for nature and foster a sense of stewardship for the environment.

6. Reduce Screen Time: Limit your use of electronic devices and make time for outdoor activities. Reducing screen time can help you be more present in the natural world and improve your overall well-being.

7. Volunteer for Conservation Efforts: Get involved in local conservation projects or volunteer for organizations that work to protect natural habitats. Volunteering not only helps the environment but

also connects you with like-minded individuals who share your passion for nature.

8. Take Nature Walks: Make it a habit to take regular nature walks, whether in a nearby park, nature reserve, or even a tree-lined street. These walks can provide a calming break from your daily routine and help you reconnect with the natural world.

9. Practice Nature Journaling: Keep a nature journal to document your observations and experiences in the outdoors. Sketch plants and animals, record your thoughts and reflections, and note any changes you observe in the environment. This practice can enhance your awareness and appreciation of nature.

10. Incorporate Nature into Your Daily Routine: Look for small ways to incorporate nature into your daily life. Open your windows to let in fresh air, take your lunch break outside, or simply sit in a park and watch the world go by. These small moments can add up to a greater sense of connection with nature.

Embracing nature is a journey that requires intention and mindfulness. By making a conscious effort to connect with the natural world, we can experience the many physical, mental, and emotional benefits it offers. Nature provides a sanctuary from the stresses of modern life, offering a space where we can find peace, inspiration, and a deeper sense of purpose.

John Muir's love for nature and his dedication to its preservation remind us of the profound impact that the natural world can have on our lives. His legacy encourages us to appreciate the beauty and wonder of nature and to take action to protect it for future generations. By following his example, we can cultivate a deeper connection to nature and experience the transformative benefits it offers.

Let the wisdom of nature guide you towards a more balanced and fulfilling life. Embrace the beauty and serenity of the natural world, and let it inspire you to live more mindfully and intentionally. The journey to simplicity is enriched by our connection to nature, and by nurturing this relationship, we can find greater happiness and well-being.

The role of nature in a simple life is indispensable. It offers a sanctuary of peace and inspiration, fostering physical health, mental clarity, and emotional well-being. The story of John Muir and his unwavering love for nature reminds us of the profound impact that the natural world can have on our lives. By incorporating practical tips for embracing nature, we can cultivate a deeper connection to the environment and experience the many benefits it provides.

Nature is a powerful ally. Take the time to immerse yourself in its beauty, appreciate its wonders, and protect its delicate balance. The more we connect with nature, the more we discover the true essence of simplicity and the profound joy that comes from living in harmony with the natural world.

## Chapter 12: Simple Living in a Modern World

In the hustle and bustle of the modern world, the concept of simple living often seems like a distant ideal. Yet, the desire to live simply and intentionally has been a guiding principle for many throughout history. Amongst the most profound and influential advocates for simple living was Henry David Thoreau, whose experiment at Walden Pond inspired generations to seek a life of simplicity, introspection, and harmony with nature.

Henry David Thoreau was born on July 12, 1817, in Concord, Massachusetts. He was a writer, philosopher, naturalist, and transcendentalist, deeply influenced by the ideas of Ralph Waldo Emerson and the transcendentalist movement. Thoreau's writings reflect his belief in the inherent goodness of nature and the value of self-reliance, individualism, and living in harmony with the natural world.

Thoreau's most famous work, "Walden; or, Life in the Woods," chronicles his experiment in simple living. In 1845, Thoreau built a small cabin on the shores of Walden Pond, near Concord, on land owned by Emerson. He lived there for two years, two months, and two days, immersing himself in nature and reflecting on the essentials of life. Thoreau's purpose was to strip away the superfluous and focus on the fundamental aspects of existence.

The Walden Pond experiment was not an escape from society but a deliberate act of living with intention and mindfulness. Thoreau sought to understand the essence of life by reducing his needs to the bare minimum and observing the natural world around him. He believed that by simplifying his life, he could gain greater clarity and insight into the human condition.

Thoreau's cabin at Walden was modest, measuring just 10 feet by 15 feet, with a single room that served as his living, working, and sleeping space. He grew much of his own food, primarily beans, potatoes, corn, and peas, and supplemented his diet with wild berries and fish from the pond. Thoreau's daily routine involved physical labour, reading, writing, and long walks in the woods, allowing him to observe the changing seasons and the rhythms of nature.

Thoreau's reflections at Walden are filled with observations about the natural world, philosophical musings, and critiques of contemporary society. He questioned the value of material wealth and the relentless pursuit of progress, advocating instead for a life of simplicity, self-sufficiency, and spiritual fulfilment. Thoreau's famous dictum, "Simplify, simplify," encapsulates his belief that true happiness and enlightenment come from focusing on the essentials and removing the distractions of modern life.

Among the key themes of "Walden" is the idea of living deliberately. Thoreau writes, "I went to the woods because I wished to live deliberately, to front only the essential facts of life, and see if I could not learn what it had to teach, and not when I came to die, discover that I had not lived." This desire to live with purpose and intention resonates deeply with the principles of simple living, reminding us to consider what is truly important in our lives.

Thoreau's experiment at Walden Pond was also a profound exploration of solitude and self-reflection. He believed that solitude was essential for personal growth and understanding, allowing individuals to connect with their inner selves and the natural world. Thoreau's time alone in the woods provided him with the space to think deeply, write extensively, and develop his philosophy of simple living.

Despite his physical isolation, Thoreau remained engaged with the world around him. He often entertained visitors at his cabin, including Emerson and other members of the transcendentalist circle.

Thoreau's writings from this period reflect a keen awareness of social and political issues, including his staunch opposition to slavery and his advocacy for civil disobedience as a means of protest.

Thoreau's legacy extends far beyond his time at Walden Pond. His writings have influenced a wide range of thinkers, activists, and movements, from Mahatma Gandhi and Martin Luther King Jr. to the modern environmental and simplicity movements. Thoreau's call to live deliberately and mindfully continues to inspire those seeking a more meaningful and intentional life.

The lessons from Thoreau's Walden experiment are particularly relevant in today's fast-paced and consumer-driven society. Here are some key takeaways from Thoreau's philosophy that can help us embrace simple living in the modern world:

1. Live Deliberately: Make conscious choices about how you spend your time and resources. Focus on what truly matters to you and align your actions with your values. Living deliberately means being intentional about your goals and priorities, rather than being swept along by the demands of society.

2. Simplify Your Possessions: Reduce the clutter in your life by letting go of unnecessary possessions. Thoreau believed that material excess distracts from the pursuit of true happiness and fulfilment. By simplifying your belongings, you can create a more organized and peaceful living space.

3. Cultivate Self-Reliance: Develop skills that allow you to be more self-sufficient. Thoreau's experiment at Walden involved growing his own food and building his own shelter. While modern life may not require such extreme measures, learning to cook, repair, and create can foster a sense of independence and accomplishment.

4. Connect with Nature: Spend time outdoors and appreciate the beauty of the natural world. Thoreau found solace and inspiration in nature, and his writings emphasize the importance of this connection. Whether it's a walk in the park, a hike in the woods, or simply sitting by a body of water, nature can provide a sense of peace and perspective.

5. Reflect and Write: Take time for introspection and self-reflection. Thoreau's writings are a testament to the power of reflection in understanding oneself and the world. Keeping a journal or writing about your thoughts and experiences can help clarify your values and goals.

6. Embrace Solitude: Find moments of solitude to recharge and reconnect with yourself. Thoreau valued solitude as a means of personal growth and introspection. In a world filled with constant noise and distractions, solitude can provide a much-needed respite.

7. Question Progress: Consider the true cost of progress and technological advancement. Thoreau

was critical of the blind pursuit of progress at the expense of the environment and individual well-being. Reflect on how modern conveniences impact your life and whether they contribute to your overall happiness.

8. Practice Mindfulness: Be present in the moment and fully engage with your surroundings. Thoreau's observations of nature were detailed and profound because he practiced mindfulness. This awareness can help you appreciate the simple joys of life and reduce stress.

9. Advocate for Change: Thoreau's commitment to social and political causes demonstrates the importance of standing up for what you believe in. Use your voice to advocate for positive change in your community and beyond. Simple living is not just about personal fulfilment but also about contributing to the greater good.

10. Value Experiences Over Possessions: Thoreau believed that experiences and personal growth were more valuable than material possessions. Focus on creating memories and learning new things rather than acquiring more stuff. This shift in perspective can lead to a more fulfilling and meaningful life.

Thoreau's Walden experiment teaches us that simple living is about more than just reducing our physical possessions. It is about cultivating a mindset of mindfulness, self-reliance, and intentionality. By embracing these principles, we can find greater clarity, peace, and fulfilment in our lives.

Henry David Thoreau's life and work offer timeless lessons on the value of simple living. His experiment at Walden Pond serves as a powerful reminder that true happiness and fulfilment come from focusing on the essentials and living with intention. Thoreau's philosophy continues to inspire those seeking a more meaningful and deliberate life in the modern world.

Why not let Thoreau's wisdom guide us towards a life of greater purpose and clarity? Embrace the lessons of Walden and discover the profound joy that comes from living simply and deliberately.

## Chapter 13: The Power of Gratitude

Gratitude is a powerful force that can transform our lives, especially when we embrace the principles of simple living. The importance of gratitude in simple living cannot be overstated. It shifts our focus from what we lack to what we have, fostering a sense of contentment and appreciation. By cultivating gratitude, we can enhance our overall well-being, strengthen our relationships, and find greater joy in the everyday moments of life.

The essence of simple living is to strip away the nonessential and focus on what truly matters. Gratitude aligns perfectly with this philosophy by encouraging us to recognize and appreciate the abundance in our lives, no matter how small. It allows us to savour the present moment, celebrate our achievements, and build a positive outlook on life. Gratitude transforms our mindset, helping us to see the beauty and blessings that surround us, even in challenging times.

Practicing gratitude daily is a simple yet profound way to enhance our quality of life. When we make gratitude a habit, we train our minds to focus on the positive aspects of our experiences, fostering resilience and optimism. Regularly acknowledging the things, we are thankful for can lead to improved mental and physical health, better sleep, and increased happiness.

Oprah Winfrey is one of the most inspiring figures who has championed the practice of gratitude. Known for her influential career in media and philanthropy, Oprah has often spoken about the transformative power of gratitude in her own life. Her gratitude practices have been a cornerstone of her success and personal fulfilment.

Oprah Winfrey's journey with gratitude began with a simple daily ritual: keeping a gratitude journal. Every day, she would write down five things she was grateful for. This practice helped her to remain grounded and focused, even during the most challenging periods of her life. Oprah credits her gratitude journal with helping her to appreciate the present moment and maintain a positive outlook, regardless of external circumstances.

Oprah's gratitude practices extend beyond her personal life. She has often shared her experiences and insights on her talk shows, encouraging millions of viewers to embrace gratitude as a way to improve their own lives. Oprah believes that gratitude is a powerful tool for personal growth and transformation, capable of shifting our perspective and opening our hearts to the abundance around us.

Oprah Winfrey's milestones in her career and personal life are a testament to the power of gratitude and perseverance. Born into poverty in rural Mississippi on January 29, 1954, Oprah faced numerous challenges during her childhood, including abuse and hardship. Despite these obstacles, she excelled in school and won a scholarship to Tennessee State University, where she studied communication.

Oprah's career in media began with a job in radio while still in high school. Her talent and charisma quickly propelled her into television, where she became the youngest and first African American woman to anchor the news at Nashville's WLAC-TV. Her breakthrough came when she moved to Chicago in 1984 to host WLS-TV's morning talk show, "AM Chicago." Within months, the show became the highest-rated talk show in the city.

In 1986, the show was renamed "The Oprah Winfrey Show," and it was nationally syndicated. The show ran for 25 years, becoming the highest-rated television talk show in history. Oprah's empathetic interviewing style, combined with her willingness to discuss personal and societal issues, resonated with millions of viewers. Her ability to connect with her audience on a deeply personal level made her a beloved and influential figure.

Beyond her talk show, Oprah's influence extended into publishing, acting, and philanthropy. She launched "O, The Oprah Magazine" in 2000, which became one of the most successful women's magazines. Her book club selections often became bestsellers, and her endorsement, known as "The Oprah Effect," could significantly boost sales and public interest.

Oprah's achievements in film and television production further showcase her versatility and impact. She founded Harpo Productions in 1988, which produced her talk show and other successful projects, including the film "The Colour Purple," in which she starred and received an Academy Award nomination. Oprah's work in film and television earned her numerous awards, including multiple Daytime Emmy Awards, a Tony Award, and the prestigious Presidential Medal of Freedom in 2013.

One of Oprah's most significant contributions has been her philanthropy. She has donated millions of dollars to educational causes, disaster relief, and initiatives to empower women and children. In 2007, she opened the Oprah Winfrey Leadership Academy for Girls in South Africa, providing high-quality education and opportunities for disadvantaged girls. Oprah's commitment to giving back and making a difference in the lives of others reflects her deep sense of gratitude and compassion.

Oprah's journey from a challenging childhood to becoming one of the most influential and wealthiest women in the world is a testament to her resilience, hard work, and gratitude. Her story inspires countless individuals to pursue their dreams, overcome obstacles, and live with intention and purpose.

To incorporate the principles of gratitude into your own life, consider these practical tips for cultivating gratitude:

1. Keep a Gratitude Journal: Like Oprah, start a daily gratitude journal. Each day, write down three to five things you are grateful for. They can be simple things, such as a beautiful sunrise, a kind gesture from a friend, or a delicious meal. Regularly reflecting on these moments can help you appreciate the positives in your life.

2. Express Gratitude to Others: Take the time to thank the people in your life who have made a difference. Whether it's a handwritten note, a heartfelt message, or a simple thank-you, expressing gratitude strengthens relationships and fosters a sense of connection.

3. Practice Mindfulness: Incorporate mindfulness practices into your daily routine to enhance your awareness of the present moment. Pay attention to the sights, sounds, and sensations around you, and appreciate the beauty and wonder of your surroundings. Mindfulness can deepen your sense of gratitude and help you stay grounded.

4. Create a Gratitude Ritual: Establish a daily or weekly ritual to celebrate and acknowledge the things you are grateful for. This could be a gratitude

walk, a family gratitude circle, or a quiet moment of reflection. Consistent rituals help reinforce the habit of gratitude.

5. Focus on Positive Affirmations: Use positive affirmations to remind yourself of the blessings in your life. Statements like "I am grateful for the love and support of my family" or "I appreciate the beauty of nature around me" can reinforce a grateful mindset.

6. Reframe Negative Experiences: When faced with challenges or setbacks, try to reframe the situation by identifying something positive or a lesson learned. This practice can help you find silver linings and maintain a grateful attitude, even in difficult times.

7. Celebrate Small Wins: Acknowledge and celebrate small achievements and milestones. Recognizing your progress, no matter how minor, can boost your motivation and sense of accomplishment. This practice reinforces the importance of appreciating the journey, not just the destination.

8. Practice Gratitude Meditation: Dedicate time to a gratitude meditation practice. Sit quietly, close your eyes, and focus on the things you are grateful for. Allow yourself to feel the warmth and positivity of gratitude, letting it fill your mind and heart.

9. Create Visual Reminders: Surround yourself with visual reminders of the things you are grateful for. Photos, quotes, and mementos can serve as daily prompts to focus on the positive aspects of your life. These reminders can help keep gratitude at the forefront of your mind.

10. Share Your Gratitude: Share your gratitude practices with others, whether through conversations, social media, or community activities. Spreading gratitude can inspire others to adopt similar practices, creating a ripple effect of positivity and appreciation.

Practising gratitude is a journey that requires consistency and intention. By making gratitude a daily habit, we can transform our mindset and cultivate a deeper sense of contentment and happiness. Gratitude helps us to focus on what truly matters, fostering a more fulfilling and meaningful life.

Oprah Winfrey's story serves as a powerful reminder of the impact that gratitude can have on our lives. Her commitment to gratitude has helped her navigate challenges, achieve success, and maintain a positive outlook. Oprah's example shows us that gratitude is not just a feeling but a practice that can be cultivated and strengthened over time.

The power of gratitude in simple living is undeniable. It shifts our focus from what we lack to what we have, fostering a sense of contentment and appreciation. By incorporating daily gratitude practices, we can enhance our well-being, strengthen our relationships, and find greater joy in the everyday moments of life.

Embrace the beauty of the present moment, celebrate your blessings, and cultivate a mindset of appreciation. The journey to simplicity is enriched by gratitude, and by nurturing this practice, we can discover the profound joy that comes from living with a grateful heart.

Gratitude is not just a passive response to positive experiences; it is an active practice that shapes our perception of the world. When we consciously choose to focus on the good, we train our minds to seek out and appreciate the positive aspects of our lives. This shift in perspective can have a profound impact on our overall well-being, helping us to feel more connected, fulfilled, and at peace.

In the chapters ahead, we will continue to explore various aspects of simple living and how they contribute to a more intentional and meaningful life. Each chapter offers insights and practical tips to help you simplify your life and find happiness in the everyday moments. Together, we will uncover the beauty and fulfilment that come from living a life of intentional simplicity and mindful gratitude.

As you integrate these practices into your life, remember that gratitude is a powerful tool for transformation. It can change our perspective, enhance our relationships and bring us closer to the essence of simple living. Embrace gratitude as a guiding principle, and let it illuminate your path towards a more fulfilling and joyful life.

By focusing on what we have, rather than what we lack, we can cultivate a sense of abundance and contentment that transcends material wealth. Gratitude reminds us that true happiness comes from within, from appreciating the beauty of the present moment and the richness of our experiences.

The power of gratitude lies in its ability to transform our lives from the inside out. By making gratitude a daily practice, we can create a more positive, fulfilling, and joyful existence. Let the spirit of gratitude infuse every aspect of your life and discover the profound impact it can have on your journey towards simple living.

Chapter 14: Simple Parenting

In a world filled with endless distractions and consumer-driven values, the concept of simple and frugal parenting offers a refreshing and meaningful approach to raising children. Simple parenting emphasizes the importance of nurturing, quality time and instilling values that focus on experiences over material possessions. By embracing simplicity and frugality in parenting, we can foster a supportive and enriching environment that promotes the well-being and development of our children.

The benefits of simple and frugal parenting are numerous. This approach helps reduce the stress and pressure often associated with modern parenting, allowing parents to focus on what truly matters—building strong, loving relationships with their children. Simple parenting encourages children to appreciate the small joys in life, develop creativity, and cultivate a sense of responsibility and independence.

Raising children with the values of simplicity involves teaching them to value experiences, relationships, and personal growth over material possessions. It means providing them with opportunities to explore their interests, develop life skills, and build meaningful connections with family and community. Simple parenting fosters resilience, empathy, and a strong sense of self-worth in children, preparing them to navigate life's challenges with confidence and grace.

One of the most inspiring examples of simple parenting can be found in the Amish community. The Amish are known for their commitment to simple living, strong family values, and a close-knit community. Their parenting approach emphasizes the importance of family, hard work, and living in harmony with nature. By examining the parenting practices of the Amish, we can gain valuable insights into how to raise children with values of simplicity and frugality.

The Amish community prioritizes family time and the development of strong family bonds. They believe that spending time together as a family is essential for building trust, communication, and mutual support. Amish families often engage in activities such as farming, cooking, and crafting, which provide opportunities for children to learn practical skills and contribute to the family's well-being.

Amish parents also place a strong emphasis on teaching their children the value of hard work and responsibility. From a young age, children are given chores and tasks that help them develop a sense of purpose and accomplishment. These responsibilities teach children the importance of contributing to the family and the community, fostering a sense of independence and self-reliance.

Education is another area where the Amish approach simplicity. Amish children attend small, community-based schools where the curriculum focuses on practical skills, basic academics, and values such as cooperation, humility, and respect. The goal is to prepare children for a life of simplicity and service, rather than one driven by competition and consumerism.

The Amish also emphasize the importance of living in harmony with nature. Children are encouraged to spend time outdoors, exploring the natural world and learning to appreciate its beauty and resources. This connection to nature fosters a sense of stewardship and responsibility for the environment, aligning with the broader values of simplicity and sustainability.

The parenting approach of the Amish community offers valuable lessons for those seeking to embrace simple and frugal parenting. Here are some practical tips to help you incorporate these principles into your own parenting style:

1. Prioritize Quality Time: Make time to connect with your children through shared activities and meaningful conversations. Focus on building strong relationships based on trust, love, and mutual respect. Quality time spent together fosters a sense of security and belonging.

2. Encourage Outdoor Play: Promote outdoor activities and exploration to help your children develop a love for nature. Outdoor play encourages physical activity, creativity, and an appreciation for the natural world. It also provides a break from screens and technology.

3. Simplify Schedules: Avoid over-scheduling your children with extracurricular activities. Allow them time for free play, relaxation, and family interactions. Simplifying schedules reduces stress and provides space for creativity and self-discovery.

4. Teach Practical Skills: Involve your children in household chores and practical tasks. Teaching them skills such as cooking, gardening, and basic repairs helps them develop independence and a sense of responsibility. These skills are valuable for their future and promote self-reliance.

5. Focus on Experiences Over Material Gifts: Prioritize experiences and quality time over material possessions. Plan family outings, camping trips, or creative projects that provide lasting memories and strengthen family bonds. Experiences are more meaningful and enriching than physical gifts.

6. Limit Screen Time: Set boundaries on the use of screens and technology. Encourage activities that promote creativity, physical activity, and face-to-face interactions. Limiting screen time helps children develop healthy habits and reduces exposure to consumerist messages.

7. Instil Values Through Storytelling: Share stories that convey important values and lessons. Whether through books, personal anecdotes, or cultural tales, storytelling is a powerful way to teach children about empathy, resilience, and the importance of simplicity.

8. Practice Gratitude: Encourage your children to practice gratitude by reflecting on the things they are thankful for. This can be done through daily conversations, journaling, or family gratitude rituals. Gratitude fosters a positive mindset and appreciation for the simple joys in life.

9. Be a Role Model: Demonstrate the values of simplicity and frugality in your own life. Children learn by observing their parents, so embodying these principles in your actions and decisions sets a powerful example. Show them the importance of living with intention and mindfulness.

10. Create a Supportive Community: Build a network of like-minded families who share your values. A supportive community provides opportunities for shared activities, mutual support,

and a sense of belonging. It reinforces the principles of simple living and strengthens family connections.

Simple and frugal parenting is not about depriving your children but about enriching their lives with meaningful experiences, strong values, and a sense of purpose. By focusing on what truly matters, you can create a nurturing environment that supports their growth and well-being.

The benefits of simple and frugal parenting are profound. This approach fosters strong family bonds, teaches valuable life skills, and instils values that prepare children for a fulfilling and intentional life. The parenting practices of the Amish community provide a powerful example of how to raise children with simplicity and purpose.

Embrace the principles of simplicity and frugality and adapt them to suit the unique needs of your family. By prioritizing what truly matters, you can create a nurturing and supportive environment that helps your children thrive.

The story of the Amish community's parenting approach offers valuable insights and inspiration for those seeking to simplify their parenting practices. By focusing on family, hard work, education, and a connection to nature, the Amish have created a way of life that fosters resilience, independence, and a deep sense of community.

Incorporating these principles into your own parenting style can lead to a more fulfilling and intentional family life. It encourages you to slow down, appreciate the small moments, and focus on what truly matters—building strong, loving relationships with your children and helping them grow into well-rounded, compassionate individuals.

As you explore the principles of simple living in this book, let the lessons of simple parenting guide you towards a more balanced and fulfilling approach to raising your children. Embrace the beauty of simplicity and discover the profound joy that comes from nurturing your children with love, intention, and mindfulness.

Remember that simple parenting is not about perfection but about making conscious choices that align with your values and support your family's well-being. By creating a nurturing environment that prioritizes relationships, experiences, and personal growth, you can help your children develop the skills and values they need to lead meaningful and fulfilling lives.

As you integrate these practices into your life, remember that parenting is a journey filled with opportunities for growth, learning, and connection. Embrace the principles of simple and frugal parenting and let them guide you towards a more meaningful and joyful family life. By focusing on what truly matters, you can create a nurturing and supportive environment that helps your children thrive and flourish.

## Chapter 15: Frugality and Creativity

Frugality and creativity are often seen as two separate concepts, but in reality, they complement each other beautifully. Living a frugal lifestyle encourages us to think outside the box and find innovative solutions to everyday challenges. By embracing frugality, we can cultivate creativity, resourcefulness, and a sense of empowerment, turning limitations into opportunities for growth and discovery.

Frugality fosters creativity by challenging us to make the most of what we have. When we operate within the constraints of a limited budget, we are forced to find new ways to meet our needs and desires. This process of problem-solving and innovation sparks creativity, as we learn to see potential in the resources available to us. Frugality encourages us to prioritize function and value over luxury and excess, leading to more thoughtful and intentional choices.

A most inspiring story of creativity born from frugality is that of J.K. Rowling, the renowned author of the Harry Potter series. Before achieving fame and fortune, Rowling faced significant financial struggles. Her journey from struggling single mother to best-selling author is a testament to the power of resilience, creativity, and the ability to turn adversity into opportunity.

J.K. Rowling's journey began in the early 1990s when she conceived the idea for Harry Potter during a delayed train journey from Manchester to London. At the time, Rowling was living on welfare benefits, struggling to make ends meet while raising her daughter as a single mother. Despite her financial hardships, Rowling was determined to pursue her passion for writing.

With limited resources, Rowling wrote much of the first Harry Potter book in cafes, where she could stay warm and save on heating costs at home. She used whatever materials she had on hand, often writing on scraps of paper and typing her manuscript on a second-hand typewriter. Rowling's frugality did not hinder her creativity; instead, it fuelled her determination to bring her imaginative world to life.

After completing the manuscript, Rowling faced numerous rejections from publishers. However, her perseverance paid off when Bloomsbury Publishing finally accepted her book. "Harry Potter and the Philosopher's Stone" was published in 1997, and the rest is history. Rowling's story is a powerful example of how creativity and frugality can lead to extraordinary success, even in the face of adversity.

Rowling's journey underscores the importance of resilience and resourcefulness in achieving our goals. Her ability to create a magical world with limited resources and her determination to succeed despite financial constraints inspire us to embrace frugality as a catalyst for creativity. By viewing limitations as opportunities for innovation, we can unlock our creative potential and find new ways to thrive.

To incorporate the principles of creative frugality into your own life, consider these practical tips for fostering creativity while living frugally:

1. Repurpose and Reuse: Look for ways to repurpose and reuse items instead of buying new ones. This can involve upcycling old furniture, using glass jars for storage, or transforming old clothing into new garments. Repurposing not only saves money but also encourages creative thinking and reduces waste.

2. DIY Projects: Embrace do-it-yourself projects to create items you need or desire. From homemade

cleaning products and cosmetics to handcrafted gifts and home decor, DIY projects allow you to personalize your belongings and develop new skills. The process of making something yourself can be deeply satisfying and cost-effective.

3. Embrace Minimalism: Adopt a minimalist mindset by focusing on quality over quantity. Choose versatile, multi-purpose items that can serve multiple functions. Simplifying your possessions can help you appreciate what you have and reduce the desire for unnecessary purchases.

4. Cook from Scratch: Cooking from scratch is a great way to save money and get creative in the kitchen. Experiment with new recipes, use seasonal ingredients and find ways to make the most of leftovers. Cooking at home not only saves money but also allows you to explore your culinary creativity.

5. Make Use of Free Resources: Take advantage of free resources in your community, such as libraries, public parks, and community events. Libraries offer a wealth of books, movies, and workshops, while parks provide a space for outdoor activities and relaxation. Community events can offer free entertainment and opportunities to connect with others.

6. Practice Mindful Spending: Be intentional about your spending by distinguishing between needs and wants. Prioritize purchases that add value to your

life and avoid impulse buys. Practising mindful spending helps you make thoughtful decisions and appreciate the value of what you have.

7. Create a Budget: Establishing a budget helps you manage your finances and identify areas where you can save money. A budget encourages you to be mindful of your expenses and find creative ways to reduce costs. Tracking your spending can also reveal patterns and opportunities for further savings.

8. Share and Borrow: Embrace the sharing economy by borrowing items you need but don't want to purchase. This can include tools, books, clothing, and even experiences. Sharing and borrowing reduce costs and foster a sense of community and cooperation.

9. Learn New Skills: Invest time in learning new skills that can help you save money and become more self-sufficient. Whether it's gardening, sewing, carpentry, or cooking, acquiring new skills empowers you to create and repair items yourself, reducing the need to buy new things.

10. Declutter Regularly: Regular decluttering helps you stay organized and prevents the accumulation of unnecessary items. By keeping only what you need and use, you can maintain a simpler, more manageable living space. Decluttering also encourages you to be mindful of future purchases and avoid unnecessary accumulation.

Creative frugality is about making the most of what you have and finding joy in the process of resourcefulness. By embracing frugality as an opportunity for innovation, you can cultivate a mindset of abundance and discover new ways to enrich your life.

The intersection of frugality and creativity offers a powerful approach to living a fulfilling and intentional life. The story of J.K. Rowling's journey before fame illustrates how creativity and resourcefulness can lead to extraordinary achievements, even in the face of financial challenges. By incorporating practical tips for creative frugality into your daily life, you can unlock your creative potential and find new ways to thrive on a budget.

While continuing to explore the principles of simple living, let the lessons of frugality and creativity guide you towards a more innovative and intentional approach to life. Embrace the challenges and opportunities that come with living frugally and discover the profound joy that comes from turning limitations into possibilities.

Creative frugality is not just about saving money; it's about cultivating a mindset of resourcefulness and resilience. By seeing potential in the resources around us and finding innovative solutions to everyday challenges, we can create a life that is rich in experiences and creativity. Frugality encourages us to be mindful of our choices and to appreciate the value of what we have, leading to a deeper sense of contentment and fulfilment.

Moving ahead, together, we will uncover the beauty and fulfilment that come from living a life of intentional simplicity and mindful creativity.

As you integrate these practices into your life, remember that creativity and frugality go hand in hand. Embrace the opportunities that come with living on a budget and let your creativity flourish. By focusing on what truly matters and making the most of what you have, you can create a life that is both fulfilling and sustainable.

In summary, the power of creative frugality lies in its ability to transform limitations into opportunities for growth and innovation. By making thoughtful and intentional choices, you can cultivate a mindset of abundance and discover the profound joy that comes from living a life of creative simplicity.

## Chapter 16: Simple Work and Productivity

In an era where busyness is often mistaken for productivity, the concept of simplicity in work offers a refreshing and effective approach to achieving meaningful results. Simple work is about focusing on what truly matters, eliminating distractions, and finding a balance that enhances both productivity and well-being. By embracing simplicity in our professional lives, we can increase efficiency, reduce stress, and create a more fulfilling work experience.

The benefits of simplicity in work are numerous. A simplified work environment fosters clarity and focus, allowing us to direct our energy towards tasks that align with our goals and values. By minimizing distractions and unnecessary complexity, we can achieve higher levels of concentration and efficiency. This approach not only enhances productivity but also promotes a sense of accomplishment and satisfaction.

One of the key principles of simple work is prioritization. It involves identifying the most important tasks and dedicating our time and resources to them. This requires a clear understanding of our goals and the ability to distinguish between urgent and important tasks. By focusing on high-priority activities, we can make significant progress towards our objectives and avoid getting bogged down by less critical tasks.

Another important aspect of simple work is the elimination of distractions. In today's digital age, we are constantly bombarded with emails, notifications, and other interruptions that can disrupt our focus. Creating a distraction-free work environment involves setting boundaries, managing technology, and developing habits that support deep work. This allows us to maintain our concentration and produce higher-quality work in less time.

Tim Ferriss, an entrepreneur, author, and advocate for simple work, offers valuable insights into achieving work-life balance through simplicity. Ferriss's approach is encapsulated in his best-selling book, "The 4-Hour Workweek," where he shares strategies for maximizing productivity while minimizing the time spent on work. His philosophy emphasizes the importance of efficiency, delegation, and focusing on what truly matters.

Ferriss's journey began with the realization that the traditional model of working long hours was not sustainable or fulfilling. He experimented with various productivity techniques and lifestyle changes, eventually developing a system that allowed him to achieve more by working less. His approach challenges conventional notions of work and encourages individuals to rethink how they allocate their time and energy.

One of the core concepts in Ferriss's approach is the principle of the Pareto Principle, also known as the 80/20 rule. This principle states that roughly 80% of results come from 20% of efforts. By identifying and focusing on the most impactful tasks, we can achieve significant outcomes with less effort. Ferriss advocates for prioritizing high-value activities and eliminating or delegating low-value tasks to free up time and resources.

Another key strategy Ferriss employs is automation. He encourages the use of technology and systems to streamline repetitive tasks and processes. By automating routine activities, we can reduce the time and effort required for mundane tasks, allowing us to focus on more meaningful work. This approach not only increases productivity but also enhances work-life balance by freeing up time for personal pursuits.

Ferriss also emphasizes the importance of delegation. Recognizing that we cannot do everything ourselves, he advocates for outsourcing tasks that can be handled by others. This allows us to leverage the skills and expertise of others while focusing our own efforts on tasks that require our unique talents and strengths. Delegation is a powerful tool for maximizing productivity and achieving a more balanced work-life dynamic.

To incorporate the principles of simple work and productivity into your own life, consider these practical tips for simplifying your work environment and increasing efficiency:

1. Prioritize Tasks: Begin each day by identifying the most important tasks that need to be accomplished. Focus on high-priority activities that align with your goals and values. Use tools like to-do lists, planners, or digital task managers to keep track of your priorities and ensure that you stay focused on what matters most.

2. Eliminate Distractions: Create a distraction-free work environment by setting boundaries and managing technology. Turn off notifications, set specific times for checking emails, and establish a dedicated workspace that minimizes interruptions. Consider using techniques like the Pomodoro Technique to structure your work time and maintain focus.

3. Streamline Processes: Look for ways to streamline and simplify your workflows. Identify repetitive tasks that can be automated or simplified. Use productivity tools and software to manage tasks, track progress, and collaborate with others. Streamlining processes reduces complexity and increases efficiency.

4. Delegate and Outsource: Recognize that you don't have to do everything yourself. Delegate tasks that can be handled by others and consider outsourcing activities that are outside your core competencies. This allows you to focus on high-value tasks and leverage the strengths of others.

5. Set Clear Goals: Establish clear, measurable goals for your work. Having specific objectives helps you stay focused and motivated. Break down larger goals into smaller, manageable tasks, and track your progress regularly. Clear goals provide direction and purpose, enhancing productivity.

6. Practice Mindfulness: Incorporate mindfulness practices into your work routine to enhance focus and reduce stress. Techniques such as meditation, deep breathing, and mindful breaks can help you stay present and maintain a calm, clear mind. Mindfulness improves concentration and helps you manage work-related stress more effectively.

7. Simplify Communication: Streamline your communication methods to reduce unnecessary emails, meetings, and messages. Use clear, concise communication to convey information efficiently. Consider using collaboration tools that facilitate effective communication and reduce the need for constant back-and-forth exchanges.

8. Implement Time Management Techniques: Utilize time management techniques such as time

blocking, the Eisenhower Matrix, or the Two-Minute Rule to organize your workday. These methods help you allocate time effectively, prioritize tasks, and avoid procrastination. Effective time management increases productivity and reduces overwhelm.

9. Create a Routine: Establish a consistent work routine that supports your productivity and well-being. A structured routine helps you build momentum, maintain focus, and create a sense of stability. Include regular breaks, exercise, and relaxation in your routine to ensure a healthy work-life balance.

10. Reflect and Adjust: Regularly reflect on your work habits and productivity strategies. Identify what is working well and areas that need improvement. Be open to adjusting your approach as needed to enhance efficiency and achieve your goals. Continuous reflection and adjustment help you stay on track and make meaningful progress.

Simple work and productivity are about finding ways to work smarter, not harder. By prioritizing what truly matters, eliminating distractions, and leveraging tools and strategies to increase efficiency, we can achieve more with less effort. This approach not only enhances productivity but also promotes a healthier work-life balance.

The benefits of simplicity in work are profound. A simplified work environment fosters clarity, focus, and efficiency, allowing us to achieve meaningful results with less effort. The story of Tim Ferriss's approach to work-life balance illustrates how embracing simplicity can lead to greater productivity and fulfilment. By incorporating practical tips for simple productivity into your daily life, you can create a work experience that is both effective and satisfying.

As we continue to explore the principles of simple living, let the lessons of simple work and productivity guide you towards a more balanced and intentional approach to your professional life. Embrace the power of simplicity and discover the profound joy that comes from focusing on what truly matters.

Simple work is not about doing less; it's about doing what matters most. By simplifying our work environment and prioritizing high-value activities, we can achieve greater results and find more satisfaction in our professional endeavours. This approach encourages us to be intentional with our time and energy, leading to a more fulfilling and balanced work life.

Tim Ferriss's journey serves as a powerful reminder that we have the ability to shape our work experience. By adopting strategies that promote efficiency, automation, and delegation, we can create a work environment that supports our goals and well-being. Ferriss's insights inspire us to rethink traditional notions of work and embrace a more innovative and intentional approach.

As you integrate these practices into your life, remember that simplicity is a powerful tool for enhancing productivity and achieving work-life balance. Embrace the opportunities that come with simplifying your work environment and let your productivity flourish. By focusing on what truly matters and making the most of your time and resources, you can create a work experience that is both effective and fulfilling.

In summary, the power of simple work and productivity lies in its ability to transform our professional lives. By making thoughtful and intentional choices, we can cultivate a mindset of efficiency and purpose, leading to a more balanced and joyful work experience. Let the principles of simple work guide you towards a more fulfilling and productive life.

## Chapter 17: Travel and Simple Living

Travelling can be one of the most enriching experiences in life, offering new perspectives, cultures, and memories. However, travel does not have to be extravagant or expensive to be meaningful. Embracing simplicity and frugality while travelling can lead to more authentic and fulfilling experiences. By focusing on what truly matters, we can enjoy travel without the burden of excess and expense.

Travelling simply and frugally involves prioritizing experiences over luxury, being mindful of our resources, and making intentional choices that align with our values. This approach not only makes travel more accessible but also allows us to connect more deeply with the places we visit and the people we meet. Simple travel encourages us to slow down, appreciate the journey, and immerse ourselves in the local culture.

One of the most influential advocates for simple and frugal travel is Rick Steves, a travel writer, television host, and guidebook author. Rick Steves' travel philosophy emphasizes the importance of cultural immersion, budget-consciousness, and meaningful experiences over superficial tourism. His approach to travel is a testament to the idea that you don't need to spend a fortune to have a rich and rewarding travel experience.

Rick Steves' journey began in the 1970s when he started leading small group tours to Europe. He quickly realized that travellers could have a more enriching experience by spending less and focusing on cultural immersion. Steves' guidebooks and television series, "Rick Steves' Europe," have since become immensely popular, providing practical advice and inspiration for travellers seeking to explore Europe on a budget.

One of the core principles of Rick Steves' travel philosophy is the idea of traveling like a local. This involves staying in locally-owned accommodations, eating at local restaurants, and using public transportation. By avoiding tourist traps and seeking out authentic experiences, travellers can gain a deeper understanding of the local culture and save money in the process.

Steves also advocates for slow travel, which means spending more time in fewer places rather than trying to see everything in a short period. Slow travel allows for a more relaxed pace, giving travellers the opportunity to truly absorb their surroundings and connect with the local way of life. This approach reduces the stress and exhaustion often associated with fast-paced travel and enhances the overall experience.

Another key aspect of Rick Steves' travel philosophy is the importance of packing light. Steves encourages travellers to bring only the essentials, emphasizing that a lighter load allows for greater mobility and flexibility. Packing light not only reduces the physical burden but also simplifies the travel experience, making it easier to navigate new destinations and focus on the experiences rather than the logistics.

To incorporate the principles of simple and frugal travel into your own adventures, consider these practical tips for enjoying travel without extravagance:

1. Plan Ahead: Research your destination thoroughly before you go. Look for budget-friendly accommodations, restaurants, and activities. Planning ahead can help you make informed decisions and avoid costly last-minute expenses.

2. Travel Off-Peak: Travel during the off-peak seasons to take advantage of lower prices and fewer crowds. Off-peak travel allows you to enjoy popular destinations without the high costs and stress associated with peak tourist season.

3. Use Public Transportation: Opt for public transportation instead of taxis or rental cars. Public transportation is often more affordable and provides an opportunity to experience the local culture. Consider walking or biking to explore your destination at a leisurely pace.

4. Stay in Local Accommodations: Choose locally-owned guesthouses, hostels, or vacation rentals instead of chain hotels. Staying in local accommodations supports the local economy and often provides a more authentic experience. Look for options that include kitchen facilities to save on dining expenses.

5. Eat Like a Local: Enjoy meals at local restaurants, street food vendors, and markets. Eating like a local is not only more affordable but also offers a taste of the regional cuisine and culture. Avoid touristy restaurants and seek out hidden gems recommended by locals.

6. Pack Light: Bring only the essentials and avoid overpacking. A lighter load makes it easier to navigate new destinations and reduces the risk of lost luggage. Focus on versatile clothing that can be mixed and matched and consider doing laundry on the go.

7. Embrace Slow Travel: Spend more time in fewer places to fully immerse yourself in the local culture. Slow travel allows you to explore at a relaxed pace, build deeper connections, and appreciate the

subtleties of your surroundings. It also reduces transportation costs and environmental impact.

8. Engage with Locals: Try to connect with local residents and learn about their way of life. Engage in conversations, participate in cultural activities, and seek out local recommendations. Building relationships with locals can lead to memorable experiences and a deeper understanding of the destination.

9. Limit Souvenir Purchases: Focus on collecting memories rather than physical souvenirs. Take photos, keep a travel journal, and savour the experiences you have. If you do buy souvenirs, choose items that are meaningful, locally made, and support the local economy.

10. Be Flexible and Open-Minded: Embrace the unexpected and be open to new experiences. Flexibility allows you to adapt to changing circumstances and make the most of your travels. Approach each day with curiosity and a sense of adventure.

Travelling simply and frugally is not about sacrificing comfort or enjoyment; it's about making intentional choices that enhance the travel experience. By focusing on cultural immersion, meaningful interactions, and budget-conscious decisions, you can create rich and rewarding travel experiences that leave a lasting impact.

The benefits of travelling simply and frugally are profound. This approach allows you to connect more deeply with the places you visit, build meaningful relationships, and create lasting memories without the burden of excess and expense. The story of Rick Steves' travel philosophy illustrates how simplicity and frugality can lead to a richer, more authentic travel experience.

As we continue to explore the principles of simple living, let the lessons of simple travel guide you towards a more intentional and fulfilling approach to exploring the world. Embrace the power of simplicity and discover the profound joy that comes from focusing on what truly matters in your travel experiences.

Travelling simply encourages us to slow down, appreciate the journey, and immerse ourselves in the local culture. It allows us to prioritize experiences over material possessions and find value in the connections we make along the way. By adopting a frugal and mindful approach to travel, we can create meaningful adventures that enrich our lives and broaden our perspectives.

Rick Steves' journey serves as a powerful reminder that travel is not about the destinations we visit, but the experiences we have and the people we meet. By embracing his principles of cultural immersion, budget-consciousness, and meaningful interactions, we can transform our travel experiences and create memories that last a lifetime.

Together, we will uncover the beauty and fulfilment that come from living a life of intentional simplicity and mindful travel.

As you integrate these practices into your life, remember that travel is a journey of discovery, not just of places but of yourself and the world around you. Embrace the opportunities that come with travelling simply, and let your adventures be guided by curiosity, mindfulness, and a sense of wonder.

To summarise, the power of simple travel lies in its ability to transform our experiences and enrich our lives. By making thoughtful and intentional choices, we can cultivate a mindset of exploration and appreciation, leading to a more fulfilling and joyful travel experience. Let the principles of simple travel guide you towards a richer, more meaningful way of exploring the world.

## Chapter 18: Simple and Frugal Hobbies

Today, where leisure activities can often be expensive and complicated, simple and frugal hobbies offer a wonderfully refreshing alternative. These hobbies are not only budget-friendly but also deeply fulfilling, allowing us to explore our interests, develop new skills, and find joy in the simplicity of everyday activities. By embracing simple and frugal hobbies, we can enrich our lives without the need for extravagant spending.

The benefits of simple hobbies are manifold. They encourage creativity, reduce stress, and provide a sense of accomplishment. Engaging in hobbies can improve mental health by offering a productive way to unwind and escape the pressures of daily life. Simple hobbies often involve activities that connect us with nature, art, and our own inner worlds, fostering a sense of peace and well-being.

Finding joy in frugal hobbies means appreciating the process and the intrinsic rewards rather than focusing on material gains or outcomes. These hobbies remind us that pleasure and satisfaction can come from the simplest of activities, whether it's tending a garden, sketching a landscape, or baking a loaf of bread. Frugal hobbies often have a slower, more mindful pace, allowing us to savour the moments and experiences they bring.

One inspiring figure who embraced simple and frugal hobbies was Beatrix Potter, the beloved author and illustrator of "The Tale of Peter Rabbit" and other cherished children's books. Potter's love for nature and art was the foundation of her creative work and personal happiness. Her story demonstrates how simple passions can lead to profound fulfilment and success.

Beatrix Potter was born in London in 1866, but she spent much of her childhood in the countryside, where she developed a deep love for nature. She enjoyed exploring the natural world, observing plants and animals, and creating detailed sketches of her findings. Potter's passion for art and nature became a lifelong pursuit, influencing her work as both an author and a conservationist.

Despite facing societal expectations that limited women's roles at the time, Potter pursued her interests with determination. She began publishing her stories and illustrations, which were initially intended for private enjoyment and sharing with friends and family. Her breakthrough came with the publication of "The Tale of Peter Rabbit" in 1902, which became an immediate success.

Potter's stories, filled with charming characters and vivid depictions of the English countryside, resonated with readers of all ages. Her meticulous attention to detail and her ability to capture the essence of nature in her illustrations were a testament to her love and respect for the natural world. Potter's simple hobbies of drawing and observing nature not only brought her personal joy but also led to a successful and enduring literary career.

Beyond her work as an author and illustrator, Beatrix Potter was also a passionate conservationist. She used the proceeds from her books to purchase and preserve farmland and natural habitats in the Lake District of England. Potter's commitment to conservation ensured that the landscapes she loved would be protected for future generations. Her legacy continues to inspire those who seek to live in harmony with nature and find fulfilment in simple pursuits.

To incorporate the principles of simple and frugal hobbies into your own life, consider these practical tips for finding joy and fulfilment in everyday activities:

1. Explore Nature: Spend time outdoors and engage in activities that connect you with nature. Whether it's hiking, birdwatching, gardening, or simply

taking a walk in the park, nature offers endless opportunities for simple and fulfilling hobbies. Observing the natural world can provide a sense of peace and inspiration.

2. Get Creative with Art: Embrace artistic hobbies such as drawing, painting, knitting, or crafting. These activities allow you to express your creativity and produce tangible results. You don't need expensive materials to get started; even simple tools can lead to beautiful creations. Art can be a therapeutic and rewarding way to spend your free time.

3. Cook and Bake at Home: Cooking and baking are practical and enjoyable hobbies that can be done on a budget. Experiment with new recipes, use seasonal ingredients, and enjoy the process of creating delicious meals and treats. Sharing your culinary creations with family and friends adds to the joy.

4. Read and Write: Reading and writing are timeless hobbies that provide endless intellectual and emotional benefits. Visit your local library to access a wealth of books for free or start a journal to capture your thoughts and experiences. Writing can be a powerful way to reflect, express yourself, and document your life.

5. Practice Mindfulness: Engage in activities that promote mindfulness and relaxation, such as yoga, meditation, or tai chi. These practices help you stay

present, reduce stress, and improve overall well-being. Mindfulness can be incorporated into any hobby, enhancing your enjoyment and appreciation of the activity.

6. Learn a Musical Instrument: Playing a musical instrument is a rewarding hobby that can bring joy and a sense of accomplishment. You don't need to invest in an expensive instrument; many affordable options are available, and second-hand instruments can be just as good. Practising music can be a relaxing and fulfilling way to spend your time.

7. Volunteer Your Time: Volunteering is a meaningful way to spend your free time while making a positive impact on your community. Find local organizations that align with your interests and offer your skills and time. Volunteering provides a sense of purpose and connection with others.

8. Engage in Physical Activity: Physical hobbies such as running, cycling, swimming, or dancing can improve your health and well-being. These activities often require minimal equipment and can be done in local parks or community centres. Regular physical activity boosts your mood and energy levels.

9. DIY Projects: Take on do-it-yourself projects that allow you to learn new skills and create something useful. From home repairs and renovations to crafting and building, DIY projects are a hands-on way to engage your creativity and resourcefulness.

These projects can also save you money and reduce waste.

10. Cultivate Relationships: Simple hobbies that involve spending time with loved ones, such as playing board games, having picnics, or engaging in shared activities, can strengthen relationships and create lasting memories. These activities are often low-cost and provide opportunities for meaningful connections.

Simple and frugal hobbies are about finding joy in the process and the intrinsic rewards they offer. By focusing on activities that resonate with your interests and values, you can create a fulfilling and balanced life without the need for extravagant spending. These hobbies remind us that the best things in life are often the simplest and most accessible.

The benefits of simple and frugal hobbies are profound. They encourage creativity, reduce stress, and provide a sense of accomplishment and joy. The story of Beatrix Potter's love for nature and art illustrates how simple hobbies can lead to a deeply fulfilling and successful life. By incorporating practical tips for simple hobbies into your daily routine, you can enrich your life and find joy in everyday activities.

As we continue to explore the principles of simple living, let the lessons of simple and frugal hobbies guide you towards a more intentional and fulfilling approach to leisure. Embrace the power of simplicity and discover the profound joy that comes from engaging in activities that resonate with your passions and values.

Simple hobbies remind us that we don't need extravagant resources to find happiness. By making intentional choices and focusing on what truly matters, we can create a life that is rich in experiences and personal growth. Whether it's through art, nature, cooking, reading, or volunteering, simple hobbies offer endless opportunities for fulfilment and joy.

Let us explore various aspects of simple living and how they contribute to a more intentional and meaningful life. Each chapter offers insights and practical tips to help you simplify your life and find happiness in the everyday moments. Together, we will uncover the beauty and fulfilment that come from living a life of intentional simplicity and mindful engagement.

As you integrate these practices into your life, remember that hobbies are not just about filling time; they are about enriching your life and connecting with your true self. Embrace the opportunities that come with simple and frugal hobbies, and let your passions guide you towards a more joyful and balanced life.

In summary, the power of simple and frugal hobbies lies in their ability to transform our leisure time into meaningful and fulfilling experiences. By making thoughtful and intentional choices, we can cultivate a mindset of creativity and appreciation, leading to a more fulfilling and joyful life. Let the principles of simple hobbies guide you towards a richer, more meaningful way of spending your free time.

## Chapter 19: Community and Simple Living

In the pursuit of a simple and fulfilling life, the role of community cannot be understated. A supportive community provides a sense of belonging, emotional support, and practical assistance, all of which are essential for well-being and happiness. Engaging with and contributing to a community enriches our lives, fostering connections that are both meaningful and enduring.

The importance of community in a simple life is multifaceted. Communities offer social interaction, shared resources, and collective wisdom. They help us navigate life's challenges and celebrate its joys, creating a network of support that enhances our resilience and sense of security. In a community, we find companionship and the opportunity to give and receive help, which are fundamental aspects of human nature.

Building and participating in a supportive community involves intentional actions and a commitment to fostering relationships. It requires us to be open, compassionate, and proactive in our interactions with others. By contributing to the well-being of our community, we not only enhance our own lives but also create a positive impact on those around us.

Remember Jane Goodall? A renowned primatologist, anthropologist, and conservationist, her work is one of the most inspiring examples of community-centred efforts. Goodall's commitment to conservation and her community-focused approach has had a profound impact on wildlife preservation and local communities around the world.

Jane Goodall's journey began in the early 1960s when she travelled to Tanzania to study chimpanzees in the wild. Her groundbreaking research revealed the complex social behaviours of chimpanzees, challenging existing scientific beliefs and raising awareness about the need to protect these intelligent creatures and their habitats. However, Goodall soon realized that conservation efforts needed to involve local communities to be truly effective.

Recognizing the interconnectedness of people and the environment, Goodall founded the Jane Goodall Institute in 1977. The institute's mission is to promote conservation through research, education, and community-centred programs. Goodall's approach emphasizes the importance of involving local communities in conservation efforts, recognizing that sustainable solutions must address both environmental and human needs.

One of the key initiatives of the Jane Goodall Institute is the TACARE (Take Care) program, which works with local communities in Africa to improve their quality of life while promoting conservation. The program focuses on sustainable agriculture, education, healthcare, and women's empowerment, demonstrating that environmental conservation and community development go hand in hand.

Through her work, Jane Goodall has shown that building strong, supportive communities is essential for achieving lasting conservation outcomes. Her efforts have empowered local communities to take an active role in protecting their environment, fostering a sense of ownership and responsibility. Goodall's holistic approach to conservation serves as a powerful example of how community involvement can drive positive change and create a sustainable future.

To incorporate the principles of community building into your own life, consider these practical tips for fostering a supportive and engaged community:

1. Get to Know Your Neighbours: Take the time to introduce yourself to your neighbours and build relationships with them. Knowing the people who live around you creates a sense of belonging and security. Simple acts of kindness, such as sharing a meal or offering help, can strengthen these connections.

2. Participate in Local Events: Attend community events, such as farmers' markets, festivals, and neighbourhood meetings. These gatherings provide opportunities to meet new people, support local businesses, and stay informed about community issues. Active participation helps you feel more connected and invested in your community.

3. Volunteer Your Time: Offer your skills and time to local organizations and causes that align with your values. Volunteering is a meaningful way to give back to your community and make a positive impact. It also allows you to meet like-minded individuals and build a network of supportive relationships.

4. Join or Form a Community Group: Consider joining or forming a group based on shared interests or goals, such as a book club, gardening group, or advocacy organization. These groups provide a sense of camaraderie and a platform for

collaborative efforts. Working together towards common objectives strengthens community bonds.

5. Support Local Businesses: Shop at local stores, eat at local restaurants, and use local services. Supporting local businesses helps sustain the local economy and fosters a sense of community pride. It also encourages more personalized and meaningful interactions with business owners and employees.

6. Engage in Community Projects: Participate in community projects, such as clean-up drives, community gardens, or neighbourhood improvement initiatives. These projects bring people together to work towards a common goal, creating a sense of shared accomplishment and pride.

7. Create Shared Spaces: Advocate for and help create shared community spaces, such as parks, community centres, and public gardens. These spaces provide areas for socializing, recreation, and community events. Shared spaces enhance the quality of life for everyone in the community and promote social interaction.

8. Practice Inclusivity: Foster an inclusive community by welcoming and respecting people from diverse backgrounds and experiences. Inclusivity creates a sense of belonging for everyone and enriches the community with a variety of perspectives and talents. Actively listen to and

support the needs and voices of all community members.

9. Communicate Openly: Maintain open and respectful communication with your community. Share information, ideas, and concerns with others, and encourage dialogue. Effective communication builds trust and helps resolve conflicts, ensuring a harmonious community environment.

10. Celebrate Together: Organize and participate in community celebrations and traditions. Whether it's a holiday gathering, a block party, or a cultural festival, celebrating together strengthens bonds and creates lasting memories. These events remind us of the joy and value of community.

Building a supportive community is a continuous process that requires effort and commitment. By taking intentional steps to connect with others and contribute to the well-being of your community, you can create a network of relationships that enrich your life and the lives of those around you.

The importance of community in a simple life is profound. A supportive community provides emotional and practical benefits that enhance our well-being and happiness. The story of Jane Goodall's community-centred conservation efforts illustrates how involving and empowering communities can lead to positive and lasting change. By incorporating practical tips for community building into your daily life, you can foster a sense of belonging and contribute to a vibrant and supportive community.

As we continue to explore the principles of simple living, let the lessons of community guide you towards a more connected and fulfilling approach to life. Embrace the power of community and discover the profound joy that comes from building and participating in a supportive network of relationships.

Community is not just about proximity; it's about connection, shared values, and mutual support. By making intentional efforts to build and nurture these connections, we can create a more compassionate and resilient society. Whether through volunteering, supporting local businesses, or simply getting to know your neighbours, every action contributes to the strength and vitality of your community.

As you integrate these practices into your life, remember that community building is an ongoing journey. Embrace the opportunities that come with being part of a community, and let your actions be guided by compassion, inclusivity, and a genuine desire to make a positive impact. By fostering a supportive community, you not only enhance your own life but also contribute to the well-being and happiness of those around you.

The power of a community lies in its ability to provide support, connection, and shared purpose. By making thoughtful and intentional choices, we can cultivate a strong and vibrant community that enriches our lives and fosters a sense of belonging. Let the principles of community guide you towards a richer, more meaningful way of living and connecting with others.

## Chapter 20: Embracing Simplicity Like Einstein

Where today's modern world is filled with distractions and materialism, the example set by Albert Einstein offers a compelling blueprint for living a life of simplicity and purpose. Known for his groundbreaking contributions to physics, Einstein's unpretentious lifestyle and philosophy of simplicity were integral to his ability to focus on his scientific work and intellectual pursuits. His approach to life emphasizes the power of simplicity and humility, illustrating how these principles can lead to profound achievements and a fulfilling existence.

Albert Einstein, born on March 14, 1879, in Ulm, Germany, is celebrated as one of the greatest scientific minds of all time. His theories of relativity revolutionized our understanding of space, time, and energy, and his work has had a lasting impact on various fields of science. Despite his monumental achievements, Einstein remained remarkably humble and lived a frugal, unpretentious life.

Einstein's lifestyle was characterized by simplicity and a deliberate focus on what truly mattered to him: his scientific inquiries and intellectual pursuits. He favoured simple clothing, often seen in a modest sweater and trousers, and avoided the social formalities and extravagances that many people of his stature might embrace. Einstein's wardrobe was practical and understated, reflecting his preference for functionality over fashion.

This minimalist approach extended beyond his wardrobe to his overall lifestyle. Einstein lived in modest homes, surrounded by books and papers, rather than luxury and opulence. He valued intellectual stimulation and personal freedom over material possessions. This simplicity allowed him to devote his energy and attention to his scientific work without the distractions of maintaining a more elaborate lifestyle.

Einstein's philosophy of simplicity was deeply intertwined with his work. He believed that simplicity was a key component of scientific inquiry, famously stating, "Everything should be made as simple as possible, but not simpler." This principle guided his approach to problem-solving, encouraging clarity and focus in both his thinking and his life.

Einstein's humble and frugal lifestyle was not merely a personal preference but a conscious choice that aligned with his values. He understood that material wealth and social status were not the true measures of success or fulfilment. Instead, he found joy and purpose in the pursuit of knowledge and the advancement of science. This focus on intellectual and spiritual wealth over material possessions is a powerful lesson for anyone seeking a more meaningful and intentional life.

Einstein's commitment to simplicity also extended to his interactions with others. He was known for his approachable and down-to-earth demeanour, treating people with kindness and respect regardless of their social status. His humility and generosity made him a beloved figure, admired not only for his scientific genius but also for his character and integrity.

To incorporate the principles of simplicity inspired by Einstein into your own life, consider these practical tips for embracing a humble and focused lifestyle:

1. Prioritize Your Passions: Focus on what truly matters to you, whether it's your career, hobbies, or personal relationships. By prioritizing your passions

and eliminating unnecessary distractions, you can lead a more fulfilling and purpose-driven life.

2. Simplify Your Wardrobe: Adopt a minimalist approach to clothing by choosing practical, comfortable, and versatile items. Simplifying your wardrobe reduces decision fatigue and allows you to focus on more important aspects of your life.

3. Live Modestly: Choose a living environment that meets your needs without excess. A modest home, free from clutter and unnecessary possessions, creates a peaceful space that supports focus and productivity.

4. Value Intellectual Pursuits: Invest your time and resources in learning and personal growth. Whether through reading, taking courses, or engaging in thoughtful discussions, prioritizing intellectual pursuits enriches your mind and soul.

5. Practice Humility: Approach life with a humble and open attitude. Recognize that everyone has something valuable to contribute and treat others with kindness and respect. Humility fosters meaningful connections and a deeper appreciation for life.

6. Reduce Materialism: Reevaluate your relationship with material possessions and focus on experiences and personal growth instead. Let go of the notion that happiness is tied to material wealth and embrace the joy of simple living.

7. Cultivate Mindfulness: Practice mindfulness to stay present and fully engage with each moment. Mindfulness helps you appreciate the simple pleasures of life and maintain a balanced, focused mindset.

8. Embrace Frugality: Adopt frugal habits that align with your values and goals. Being mindful of your spending and resource use allows you to live sustainably and with greater financial freedom.

9. Create a Simple Environment: Surround yourself with simplicity by decluttering your living and working spaces. A clean, organized environment supports mental clarity and productivity.

10. Pursue Lifelong Learning: Commit to continuous learning and personal development. Embrace curiosity and seek knowledge in all areas of life, just as Einstein did throughout his remarkable career.

Einstein's life teaches us that simplicity is not a limitation but a powerful tool for achieving greatness and fulfilment. By focusing on what truly matters and eliminating the superfluous, we can create a life that is both meaningful and impactful. Einstein's example inspires us to prioritize intellectual and spiritual growth over material wealth, reminding us that true success comes from within.

The simplicity and humility of Albert Einstein's lifestyle offer valuable lessons for those seeking a more intentional and fulfilling life. His unpretentious approach to living and his unwavering focus on his passions illustrate the profound benefits of simplicity. By incorporating the principles of simplicity inspired by Einstein into your own life, you can create a more balanced, purposeful, and joyful existence.

Let Einstein's example guide you towards a more focused and meaningful approach to life. Embrace the power of simplicity and discover the profound joy that comes from living with intention and clarity.

## Chapter 21: Leonardo da Vinci: Simplicity and Genius

Leonardo da Vinci, one of history's most brilliant minds, epitomizes the union of simplicity and genius. Known for his remarkable contributions to art, science, and invention, da Vinci led a frugal and minimalist lifestyle that allowed him to focus intensely on his intellectual and creative pursuits. His life and teachings offer valuable insights into how simplicity can foster extraordinary achievements and a deeply fulfilling existence.

Born on April 15, 1452, in Vinci, Italy, Leonardo da Vinci displayed an insatiable curiosity and a diverse range of talents from a young age. His interests spanned painting, sculpture, engineering, anatomy, and more. Despite his many skills and accomplishments, da Vinci chose to live modestly, directing his resources towards his work and studies rather than material possessions.

Da Vinci's frugality was evident in his everyday life. He often lived in humble quarters, valuing functionality and simplicity over luxury. This minimalist approach extended to his diet as well; da Vinci was known for his vegetarianism, a practice uncommon in his time. He believed in the ethical treatment of animals and saw a plant-based diet as a way to live harmoniously with nature.

Leonardo's simple lifestyle was not only a matter of personal preference but also a strategic choice that enabled him to devote more time and energy to his intellectual and artistic endeavours. By minimizing distractions and material needs, he could focus on what truly mattered to him: the pursuit of knowledge and the perfection of his craft.

One of da Vinci's most significant teachings is the idea that simplicity is the ultimate sophistication. This philosophy is reflected in his art and inventions, where he sought to distil complex ideas and forms into their most essential and elegant expressions. Whether through the delicate smile of the Mona Lisa or the intricate designs of his engineering sketches, da Vinci's work exemplifies the beauty and power of simplicity.

Leonardo's pursuit of intellectual and artistic excellence was driven by relentless curiosity and a dedication to lifelong learning. He believed that knowledge and creativity were interconnected and that a true understanding of the world required a holistic approach. This interdisciplinary mindset led him to study a wide range of subjects, from anatomy and physiology to physics and mathematics, often recording his observations and ideas in detailed notebooks.

These notebooks, filled with sketches, scientific diagrams, and written reflections, reveal the depth and breadth of da Vinci's inquiries. They also showcase his ability to see connections between seemingly unrelated fields, demonstrating his belief that all knowledge is interconnected. Leonardo's holistic approach to learning and his emphasis on the interconnectedness of all things remain influential to this day.

Da Vinci's frugal and minimalist lifestyle extended to his approach to time management and productivity. He was known for his meticulous planning and his ability to focus intensely on his work. By prioritizing his artistic and scientific pursuits over social obligations and material distractions, Leonardo was able to achieve a level of mastery and innovation that few have matched.

To incorporate the principles of simplicity inspired by Leonardo da Vinci into your own life, consider these practical tips for embracing a minimalist and dedicated lifestyle:

1. Focus on What Matters: Identify your core passions and dedicate your time and resources to pursuing them. By prioritizing what truly matters to

you, you can achieve greater fulfilment and success in your chosen fields.

2. Live Modestly: Adopt a minimalist approach to your living environment. Choose functionality and simplicity over luxury and excess. A modest living space can provide a peaceful and focused atmosphere that supports your goals.

3. Simplify Your Diet: Consider a simple and ethical approach to your diet. A plant-based or minimalist diet can promote health and well-being while reducing your impact on the environment. Focus on natural, whole foods that nourish your body and mind.

4. Cultivate Curiosity: Embrace a mindset of lifelong learning and curiosity. Explore a wide range of subjects and seek connections between different fields of knowledge. This holistic approach can lead to innovative ideas and a deeper understanding of the world.

5. Practice Mindfulness: Incorporate mindfulness practices into your daily routine to enhance focus and clarity. Techniques such as meditation, deep breathing, and mindful observation can help you stay present and fully engage with your work.

6. Keep Detailed Records: Document your observations, ideas, and progress in a journal or notebook. Like da Vinci's notebooks, these records can serve as a valuable resource for reflection and

inspiration. Regular documentation helps you track your growth and refine your understanding.

7. Embrace Simplicity in Art: Whether you are an artist, writer, or creator, strive for simplicity and elegance in your work. Focus on the essential elements that convey your message or vision most effectively. Simplicity can enhance the impact and beauty of your creations.

8. Prioritize Intellectual Growth: Dedicate time to intellectual pursuits and personal development. Engage in activities that challenge your mind and expand your knowledge. This commitment to growth fosters creativity and innovation.

9. Limit Distractions: Create a work environment that minimizes distractions and supports deep focus. Set boundaries for technology use and social interactions to ensure that you can concentrate fully on your tasks. A distraction-free environment enhances productivity and creativity.

10. Find Balance: While dedication to your passions is important, also ensure that you maintain a balance between work and rest. Allow time for relaxation, reflection, and self-care. A balanced lifestyle supports sustained creativity and well-being.

Leonardo da Vinci's life teaches us that simplicity and focus are powerful tools for achieving greatness. By embracing a minimalist lifestyle and dedicating ourselves to our passions, we can unlock our full potential and make meaningful contributions to the world. Da Vinci's example inspires us to live with intention, pursue knowledge, and create with purpose.

The simplicity and dedication of Leonardo da Vinci's lifestyle offer valuable lessons for those seeking a more intentional and fulfilling life. His frugal approach and relentless pursuit of excellence illustrate the profound benefits of simplicity. By incorporating the principles of simplicity inspired by da Vinci into your own life, you can create a more focused, purposeful, and joyful existence.

Exploring the principles of simple living, let da Vinci's example guide you towards a more dedicated and meaningful approach to life. Embrace the power of simplicity and discover the profound joy that comes from living with clarity and purpose.

Leonardo da Vinci's legacy extends far beyond his masterpieces and inventions. His philosophy of simplicity, curiosity, and dedication continues to inspire countless individuals across various fields. By adopting his approach to life, we can cultivate a mindset that prioritizes intellectual growth, creativity, and a harmonious relationship with the world around us.

While integrating these practices into our lives, it is imperative to remember that simplicity is not about depriving yourself but about focusing on what truly matters. Embrace the lessons of Leonardo da Vinci and let them guide you towards a life of purpose, creativity, and fulfilment. By simplifying your surroundings, prioritizing your passions, and cultivating a mindset of curiosity and dedication, you can achieve great things and live a life that is both meaningful and inspired.

In essence, the power of simplicity lies in its ability to foster clarity, focus, and creativity. By making thoughtful and intentional choices, we can cultivate a lifestyle that supports our highest aspirations and deepest values. Let the principles of simplicity and dedication inspired by Leonardo da Vinci guide you towards a richer, more meaningful way of living.

## Chapter 22: Living a Life of Compassion Like Mother Teresa

Mother Teresa, known as Saint Teresa of Calcutta, is a shining example of how a life dedicated to simplicity, humility, and selfless service can have a profound impact on the world. Her modest lifestyle and unwavering commitment to helping the poorest of the poor reflect the deep compassion and love that guided her every action. Mother Teresa's life and teachings offer valuable lessons on the power of compassion and the importance of serving others over the pursuit of material wealth.

Born Anjezë Gonxhe Bojaxhiu on August 26, 1910, in Skopje, Macedonia, Mother Teresa felt a calling to religious life at a young age. She joined the Sisters of Loreto, an Irish community of nuns with missions in India, and took the name Teresa after Saint Thérèse of Lisieux. In 1929, she arrived in India, where she spent nearly 20 years teaching at St. Mary's High School in Calcutta.

In 1946, during a train journey to the Loreto convent in Darjeeling, Mother Teresa experienced what she later described as the "call within the call." She felt a deep urging to leave the convent and live among the poorest of the poor, dedicating herself to their service. This calling led her to establish the Missionaries of Charity in 1950, a religious congregation committed to serving the sick, destitute, and dying.

Mother Teresa's lifestyle was marked by simplicity and modesty. She owned very few personal possessions, choosing instead to focus on the well-being of others. Her simple white sari with blue borders became a symbol of her commitment to poverty and humility. She lived among those she served, sharing their hardships and providing comfort and care with unwavering dedication.

Her philosophy of life was centred on the power of compassion, love, and selfless service. Mother Teresa believed that true wealth was found in the ability to give and love unconditionally. She often spoke about the importance of small acts of kindness, emphasizing that even the smallest gesture of love could make a significant difference in someone's life. Her famous quote, "Not all of us can do great things. But we can do small things with great love," encapsulates this belief.

Mother Teresa's work was not limited to providing physical care; she also offered emotional and spiritual support to those in need. She believed that every person deserved to die with dignity and love, and she established hospices where the terminally ill could receive compassionate care in their final days. Her efforts extended to orphanages, leprosy clinics, and homes for the mentally ill, always driven by her deep compassion and commitment to alleviating suffering.

The most powerful aspect of Mother Teresa's philosophy was her emphasis on seeing the face of God in every person she encountered. She taught that serving others was a way of serving God and that each act of kindness was an expression of divine love. This spiritual perspective gave her the strength and resilience to continue her work despite the immense challenges and obstacles she faced.

To incorporate the principles of compassion and simplicity inspired by Mother Teresa into your own life, consider these practical tips for living a life of selfless service and humility:

1. Practice Kindness: Perform small acts of kindness every day. Whether it's offering a smile, a kind word, or a helping hand, these simple gestures can have a profound impact on those around you. Kindness is a powerful way to connect with others and spread positivity.

2. Live Modestly: Adopt a lifestyle that prioritizes needs over wants. Focus on living simply and avoiding unnecessary material possessions. A modest lifestyle allows you to direct your resources

towards helping others and supporting causes that matter to you.

3. Volunteer Your Time: Dedicate time to volunteer for organizations that serve the needy. Whether it's working at a food bank, a homeless shelter, or a community centre, volunteering is a way to give back to your community and make a tangible difference in the lives of others.

4. Offer Emotional Support: Be present for those who are struggling emotionally or mentally. Sometimes, a listening ear or a comforting presence is all that is needed to provide solace. Show empathy and compassion to those who are going through difficult times.

5. Focus on Small Acts: Remember that even small actions can have a significant impact. Don't underestimate the power of simple gestures like offering a meal to someone in need or writing a note of encouragement to a friend. These acts of love and kindness accumulate to create meaningful change.

6. Embrace Humility: Approach life with humility and an open heart. Recognize that everyone has something valuable to offer and treat others with respect and dignity. Humility fosters deeper connections and helps you see the inherent worth in every individual.

7. Create a Supportive Community: Build and participate in a community that values compassion

and service. Surround yourself with like-minded individuals who share your commitment to making a positive difference. A supportive community can amplify your efforts and provide mutual encouragement.

8. Practice Gratitude: Cultivate a sense of gratitude for the blessings in your life. Gratitude helps you focus on the positives and reinforces the importance of giving back. By appreciating what you have, you become more motivated to share with others.

9. Advocate for Change: Use your voice to advocate for policies and initiatives that support the marginalized and vulnerable. Whether through activism, writing, or public speaking, advocating for change is a powerful way to contribute to social justice and equity.

10. Reflect and Grow: Regularly reflect on your actions and their impact. Consider how you can continue to grow in compassion and service. Personal reflection helps you stay aligned with your values and identify areas for further development.

Mother Teresa's life teaches us that true fulfilment comes from serving others with love and humility. Her example inspires us to look beyond ourselves and dedicate our lives to the well-being of others. By embracing the principles of compassion, simplicity, and selfless service, we can create a more just and loving world.

The simplicity and compassion of Mother Teresa's lifestyle offer valuable lessons for those seeking a more intentional and fulfilling life. Her dedication to serving the poorest of the poor and her emphasis on small acts of kindness illustrate the profound impact of selfless love. By incorporating the principles of compassion and humility inspired by Mother Teresa into your own life, you can create a more meaningful and joyful existence.

As we continue to explore the principles of simple living, let Mother Teresa's example guide you towards a life of selfless service and deep compassion. Embrace the power of love and humility and discover the profound joy that comes from making a positive difference in the lives of others.

Mother Teresa's legacy extends far beyond her individual acts of kindness. Her philosophy of seeing the divine in every person and her unwavering commitment to alleviating suffering continue to inspire people around the world. By adopting her approach to life, we can cultivate a mindset that prioritizes compassion, service, and the well-being of others.

Simplicity and compassion are not just about what we give up but about what we gain. Embrace the lessons of Mother Teresa and let them guide you towards a life of purpose, love, and fulfilment. By focusing on what truly matters and dedicating yourself to the service of others, you can achieve great things and live a life that is both meaningful and inspired.

The power of compassion lies in its ability to transform lives and create lasting change. By making thoughtful and intentional choices, we can cultivate a lifestyle that supports our highest aspirations and deepest values. Let the principles of compassion and humility inspired by Mother Teresa guide you towards a richer, more meaningful way of living.

## Chapter 23: Sustaining a Simple and Frugal Life

Maintaining a simple and frugal life is an ongoing journey that requires dedication, mindfulness, and resilience. While the initial transition to simplicity and frugality can be refreshing and rewarding, sustaining these principles long-term can present unique challenges and setbacks. By reflecting on the lives of notable advocates for simple living and incorporating practical strategies, we can navigate these challenges and continue to enjoy the benefits of a simplified lifestyle.

The essence of sustaining simplicity and frugality lies in staying true to your core values and continuously adapting to new circumstances. It's about making intentional choices that align with your goals and finding joy in the process. Over time, the practices of simplicity and frugality become ingrained habits, guiding you towards a more fulfilling and purposeful life.

A key challenge in maintaining a simple and frugal life is resisting societal pressures and consumerist temptations. In a world that often equates success with material wealth and constant consumption, staying committed to simplicity requires a strong sense of self-awareness and determination. It's important to remind ourselves of the reasons we chose this path and the benefits it brings to our lives.

Overcoming setbacks is another critical aspect of sustaining simplicity and frugality. Life is unpredictable, and unexpected events can disrupt your plans and routines. Whether it's a financial setback, a change in circumstances, or a moment of weakness, it's essential to approach these challenges with flexibility and resilience. Adaptability and a positive mindset can help you navigate setbacks and stay focused on your long-term goals.

Reflecting on the lives of simple living advocates can provide inspiration and practical insights for sustaining a simple and frugal life. Individuals like Mahatma Gandhi, Thoreau, and Mother Teresa exemplify the enduring power of simplicity and frugality. Their commitment to these principles, even in the face of adversity, serves as a powerful reminder of the profound impact that a simple life can have on personal well-being and the world at large.

To sustain simplicity and frugality long-term, consider these practical tips and strategies:

1. Set Clear Goals: Define what simplicity and frugality mean to you and set specific, achievable

goals. Having clear objectives helps you stay focused and motivated. Revisit and adjust your goals periodically to ensure they remain relevant and aligned with your values.

2. Create a Supportive Environment: Surround yourself with like-minded individuals who share your commitment to simplicity and frugality. A supportive community can provide encouragement, accountability, and inspiration. Engage in discussions, share experiences, and learn from each other.

3. Embrace Mindfulness: Practice mindfulness to stay present and aware of your choices. Mindfulness helps you make intentional decisions, appreciate the present moment, and avoid impulsive actions. Techniques such as meditation, journaling, and mindful breathing can enhance your mindfulness practice.

4. Prioritize Needs Over Wants: Focus on fulfilling your essential needs rather than succumbing to wants and desires. Distinguish between what is necessary and what is superfluous. This mindset helps you avoid unnecessary purchases and maintain a frugal lifestyle.

5. Simplify Your Finances: Manage your finances with simplicity and frugality in mind. Create a budget, track your expenses, and identify areas where you can reduce costs. Consider adopting practices such as saving a portion of your income,

avoiding debt, and investing in long-term financial security.

6. Cultivate Gratitude: Develop a habit of gratitude to appreciate the simple pleasures in life. Gratitude shifts your focus from what you lack to what you have, fostering contentment and satisfaction. Regularly reflect on the positive aspects of your life and express gratitude for them.

7. Declutter Regularly: Make decluttering a regular practice to maintain a simple living environment. Periodically assess your belongings and let go of items that no longer serve a purpose or bring joy. A clutter-free space enhances mental clarity and reduces stress.

8. Learn and Adapt: Continuously seek knowledge and adapt to new circumstances. Stay informed about sustainable practices, frugal living strategies, and minimalist principles. Be open to experimenting with new ideas and adjusting your approach as needed.

9. Find Joy in Simple Activities: Engage in hobbies and activities that bring you joy without requiring significant financial investment. Gardening, reading, cooking, hiking, and crafting are examples of simple and fulfilling pursuits. Finding joy in these activities reinforces the value of a simple and frugal life.

10. Reflect on Your Progress: Regularly reflect on your journey and assess your progress towards sustaining simplicity and frugality. Acknowledge your achievements, identify areas for improvement, and celebrate the positive changes in your life. Reflection helps you stay connected to your values and goals.

Reflecting on the stories of simple living advocates can provide valuable insights and motivation. For instance, Mahatma Gandhi's unwavering commitment to simplicity and self-sufficiency, even in the face of immense challenges, serves as a powerful example of the impact that a simple life can have. His dedication to non-violence, truth, and self-reliance continues to inspire individuals around the world.

Similarly, the writings of Henry David Thoreau, particularly "Walden," offer timeless lessons on the benefits of living simply and in harmony with nature. Thoreau's experiment in simple living at Walden Pond demonstrates the profound connection between simplicity and personal fulfilment.

Mother Teresa's life of selfless service and humility further exemplifies the power of simplicity. Her unwavering focus on helping the poorest of the poor, despite limited resources, highlights the profound impact that compassion and love can have on the world.

By drawing inspiration from these individuals and incorporating practical strategies into your daily life, you can sustain a simple and frugal lifestyle that brings long-term benefits and fulfilment. Remember that simplicity and frugality are not about deprivation but about making intentional choices that align with your values and goals.

Maintaining simplicity and frugality long-term requires dedication, mindfulness, and resilience. By setting clear goals, creating a supportive environment, and embracing mindfulness, you can navigate challenges and stay committed to your principles. Reflecting on the lives of simple living advocates provides valuable insights and inspiration for sustaining a simple and frugal life.

As we continue to explore the principles of simple living, let the lessons of these advocates guide you towards a more intentional and fulfilling approach to life. Embrace the power of simplicity and discover the profound joy that comes from living with clarity and purpose.

Sustaining a simple and frugal life is a journey that evolves over time. By making thoughtful and intentional choices, you can create a lifestyle that supports your highest aspirations and deepest values. Let the principles of simplicity and frugality guide you towards a richer, more meaningful way of living.

In summary, the power of simplicity lies in its ability to foster clarity, focus, and resilience. By incorporating practical tips and drawing inspiration from simple living advocates, you can sustain a lifestyle that brings long-term benefits and fulfilment. Embrace the journey of simplicity and frugality, and let it guide you towards a more purposeful and joyful life.

## Conclusion

Embracing the Beauty of Simple and Frugal Living

As we conclude our journey through the principles of simple and frugal living, it's time to reflect on the key messages and insights we've explored. Throughout this book, we've examined how simplicity and frugality can lead to a more fulfilling, purposeful, and joyful life. By focusing on what truly matters and making intentional choices, we can create a lifestyle that nurtures our well-being and aligns with our deepest values.

One central theme of this book is the importance of prioritizing experiences, relationships, and personal growth over material possessions. Living simply allows us to strip away the excess and focus on the essentials, leading to greater clarity and contentment. Frugality encourages us to be mindful of our resources and to find creative solutions to meet our needs without unnecessary spending.

The stories of notable figures such as Mahatma Gandhi, Henry David Thoreau, Mother Teresa, and Leonardo da Vinci illustrate the profound impact that simplicity and frugality can have on our lives and the world around us. These individuals exemplify how a commitment to simple living can lead to extraordinary achievements, deep personal fulfilment, and lasting contributions to society.

In the chapters on simplicity and frugality, we've explored practical strategies for decluttering our lives, managing our finances, and embracing sustainable living. We've learned about the psychological and emotional benefits of mindfulness, gratitude, and minimalism. We've also delved into the joys of simple hobbies, the importance of community, and the power of selfless service.

Reflecting on these insights, it's clear that simplicity and frugality are not about deprivation but about making intentional choices that enhance our quality of life. By focusing on what truly matters, we can create a life that is rich in experiences, relationships, and personal growth. The journey towards simplicity is ongoing and evolves with time, requiring mindfulness, dedication, and resilience.

Living a simple and frugal life offers numerous benefits, including reduced stress, increased financial security, and a greater sense of purpose and satisfaction. It allows us to be more present in the moment, appreciate the beauty of everyday experiences, and build deeper connections with the people around us. By adopting these principles, we can lead a more balanced, harmonious, and meaningful life.

As you continue your journey towards simplicity and frugality, remember to be patient and kind to yourself. Change takes time, and it's important to celebrate your progress and learn from any setbacks. Stay true to your values, prioritize what truly matters, and remain open to new insights and experiences. By doing so, you'll cultivate a lifestyle that supports your well-being and aligns with your aspirations.

The key message of this book emphasizes the profound impact of simplicity and frugality on our lives. By embracing these principles, we can create a life that is more intentional, fulfilling, and joyful. The stories of inspiring figures and the practical tips provided offer valuable guidance for navigating the challenges and opportunities of simple living.

**Final Thoughts on Living a Simple and Frugal Life**

As we wrap up our exploration of simple and frugal living, it's important to acknowledge that this journey is deeply personal and unique for each individual. There is no one-size-fits-all approach, and the path to simplicity may look different for everyone. What matters most is that you find a way of living that resonates with your values and brings you happiness and fulfilment.

Living simply and frugally is about making conscious choices that reflect your priorities and values. It's about recognizing that true wealth lies not in material possessions but in the richness of our experiences, relationships, and personal growth. By focusing on what truly matters, we can create a life that is deeply meaningful and rewarding.

## Closing Remarks

As you embark on or continue your journey towards a simple and frugal life, take inspiration from the stories and insights shared in this book. Remember that the greatest achievements often come from humble beginnings, and the most profound joys can be found in the simplest of moments. Embrace the beauty of simplicity and let it guide you towards a life filled with purpose, love, and fulfilment.

May you find joy in the small things, peace in simplicity, and strength in the knowledge that you are living in alignment with your values. May your journey be filled with moments of clarity, connection, and contentment. And may you inspire others to embrace the power of simplicity and frugality in their own lives.

The path to a simple and frugal life is a journey of discovery, growth, and transformation. By making intentional choices and focusing on what truly matters, you can create a life that is rich in meaning and joy. As you move forward, let the principles of simplicity and frugality be your guiding lights, illuminating the way towards a brighter, more fulfilling future.

Thank you for joining me on this journey. May your life be filled with the beauty and peace of simplicity, and may you continue to find inspiration and fulfilment in the practice of living simply and frugally.

**Epilogue: The Joy of Less**

Coming to the end of this journey through the principles and practices of simple and frugal living, I hope you have found inspiration, guidance, and encouragement to embrace simplicity in your own life. "The Joy of Less: Embrace Simplicity for a Happy & Fulfilled Life" is more than just a collection of ideas; it is a call to action, inviting you to redefine your relationship with possessions, time, and the world around you.

Throughout this book, we have explored the profound impact that simplicity and frugality can have on our well-being and happiness. We have delved into the lives of remarkable individuals like Mahatma Gandhi, Mother Teresa, Leonardo da Vinci, and others who exemplified the power of living with less and focusing on what truly matters. Their stories serve as powerful reminders that a life of simplicity is not about deprivation but about abundance—abundance of purpose, connection, and joy.

Living a simple and frugal life is an ongoing journey that evolves with time and experience. It requires mindfulness, intentionality, and a willingness to let go of societal pressures and consumerist temptations. It calls for a shift in mindset, where we prioritize experiences, relationships, and personal growth over material possessions.

As you continue to navigate this path, remember that simplicity is a deeply personal and unique journey. There is no one-size-fits-all approach, and it is essential to find what resonates with you and aligns with your values. Embrace the process of discovery and allow yourself the freedom to adapt and grow.

The joy of less is found in the small, everyday moments of clarity and contentment. It is in the peace of a decluttered space, the satisfaction of a well-managed budget, the pleasure of a simple meal shared with loved ones, and the fulfilment of a life lived with purpose. By focusing on what truly matters, you can create a life that is rich in meaning and joy.

As you move forward, may you continue to find inspiration in the principles of simplicity and frugality. May you cultivate mindfulness, gratitude, and resilience, and may you share the beauty of less with those around you. Remember that the greatest wealth is not in what we possess but in the richness of our experiences, relationships, and inner peace.

Thank you for joining me on this journey. May your life be filled with the joy of less, and may you continue to embrace simplicity for a happy and fulfilled life.

## References

Books and Publications:

1. Gandhi, M. K. The Story of My Experiments with Truth. Beacon Press, 1957.
2. Thoreau, Henry David. Walden; or Life in the Woods. Ticknor and Fields, 1854.
3. Einstein, Albert. Ideas and Opinions. Crown Publishers, 1954.
4. Mother Teresa. Come Be My Light: The Private Writings of the "Saint of Calcutta". Doubleday, 2007.
5. Da Vinci, Leonardo. The Notebooks of Leonardo Da Vinci. Edited by Irma A. Richter, Oxford University Press, 2008.
6. Pollan, Michael. In Defense of Food: An Eater's Manifesto. Penguin Press, 2008.
7. Ramsey, Dave. The Total Money Makeover: A Proven Plan for Financial Fitness. Thomas Nelson, 2003.

8. Ferriss, Timothy. The 4-Hour Workweek: Escape 9-5, Live Anywhere, and Join the New Rich. Crown Publishers, 2007.
9. Kondo, Marie. The Life-Changing Magic of Tidying Up: The Japanese Art of Decluttering and Organizing. Ten Speed Press, 2014.
10. Steves, Rick. Europe Through the Back Door. Avalon Travel Publishing, 1980.


Articles and Journals:

1. Goodall, Jane. "In the Shadow of Man." National Geographic, May 1971.
2. Winfrey, Oprah. "What I Know For Sure." O, The Oprah Magazine, October 2000.
3. Babauta, Leo. "The Simple Guide to a Minimalist Life." Zen Habits, April 2010.
4. Potter, Beatrix. "The Tale of Peter Rabbit." Frederick Warne & Co., 1902.
5. Shiva, Vandana. "Earth Democracy: Justice, Sustainability, and Peace." South End Press, 2005.
6. The Minimalists (Millburn, Joshua Fields, and Nicodemus, Ryan). "Minimalism: Live a Meaningful Life." Asymmetrical Press, 2011.
7. Chouinard, Yvon. "Let My People Go Surfing: The Education of a Reluctant Businessman." Penguin Books, 2005.

Websites and Online Resources:

1. The Jane Goodall Institute. "Our Mission and Vision." janegoodall.org.

2. The Dave Ramsey Show. "Financial Peace University." daveramsey.com.
3. Rick Steves' Europe. "Travel Tips and Resources." ricksteves.com.
4. Zen Habits. "Simplify Your Life." zenhabits.net.
5. Marie Kondo. "KonMari Method." konmari.com.
6. Patagonia. "Environmental Responsibility." patagonia.com.
7. The Minimalists. "Minimalism: A Documentary About the Important Things." theminimalists.com.

Quotes and Speeches:

1. Gandhi, M. K. "Live as if you were to die tomorrow. Learn as if you were to live forever."
2. Thoreau, Henry David. "Simplify, simplify."
3. Einstein, Albert. "Everything should be made as simple as possible, but not simpler."
4. Mother Teresa. "Not all of us can do great things. But we can do small things with great love."
5. Leonardo da Vinci. "Simplicity is the ultimate sophistication."

Documentaries and Films:

1. "Gandhi." Directed by Richard Attenborough, Columbia Pictures, 1982.
2. "The Minimalists: Less Is Now." Directed by Matt D'Avella, Netflix, 2021.
3. "Jane." Directed by Brett Morgen, National Geographic Documentary Films, 2017.
4. "Jiro Dreams of Sushi." Directed by David Gelb, Magnolia Pictures, 2011.

5. "Let My People Go Surfing." Directed by Tom Campion, Patagonia Films, 2006.

Additional References:

1. The World Bank. "World Development Report 2019: The Changing Nature of Work."
2. United Nations. "Sustainable Development Goals."
3. Environmental Protection Agency (EPA). "Sustainable Practices for Home and Community."
4. Harvard Business Review. "The Benefits of Minimalism in Business."

## Acknowledgements

Creating "The Joy of Less: Embrace Simplicity for a Happy & Fulfilled Life" has been a journey of inspiration, learning, and gratitude. I would like to extend my heartfelt thanks to the many individuals who have contributed to the development of this book.

First and foremost, my deepest appreciation goes to the remarkable individuals whose lives and philosophies have provided the foundation for this work. Mahatma Gandhi, Mother Teresa, Leonardo da Vinci, and so many others—your dedication to simplicity and frugality continues to inspire and guide us all.

I am grateful to my family and friends for their unwavering support and encouragement throughout this project. Your belief in the value of simplicity and your constant love have been invaluable.

Finally, I extend my gratitude to the readers. Your interest in embracing a simple and frugal life is a testament to the enduring appeal and profound benefits of this way of living. May this book serve as a guide and inspiration on your journey toward a happier and more fulfilled life.

## Copyright Information

The Joy of Less: Embrace Simplicity for a Happy & Fulfilled Life

## © 2024 Dr Bhaskar Bora

## Legal Disclaimer

The information contained in "The Joy of Less: Embrace Simplicity for a Happy & Fulfilled Life" is provided for informational purposes only and is not intended as a substitute for the advice provided by your physician or other healthcare professional, financial advisor, or any other professional.

While the author has made every effort to ensure the accuracy and completeness of the information contained in this book, the author and publisher assume no responsibility for errors, inaccuracies, omissions, or any other inconsistencies herein. Any reliance you place on such information is strictly at your own risk.

The author and publisher disclaim any liability, loss, or risk incurred as a consequence, directly or indirectly, from the use and application of any of the contents of this book. The reader is encouraged to consult appropriate professionals for advice tailored to their individual circumstances.

The examples and stories presented in this book are for illustrative purposes only. They should not be considered as definitive or universally applicable. The experiences and results of individuals may vary, and past success is not a guarantee of future results.

By reading this book, you acknowledge that you are responsible for your own decisions and actions and that the author and publisher cannot be held liable for any outcomes resulting from the use of the information provided.